OTHER BOOKS BY THE AUTHORS

Edited by Joey Anuff
*Suck: Worst-Case Scenarios in Media, Culture, Advertising,
and the Internet* (with Ann Marie Cox)

By Gary Wolf
Aether Madness (with Michael Stein)

DUMB MONEY

DUMB
ADVENTURES OF A DAY TRADER
MONEY

JOEY ANUFF
AND
GARY WOLF

RANDOM HOUSE
NEW YORK

RANDOM HOUSE and colophon are registered trademarks
of Random House, Inc.

Library of Congress Cataloging-in-Publication Data
Anuff, Joey.
Dumb money: adventures of a day trader / Joey Anuff and Gary Wolf.
p. cm.
Includes index.
ISBN 0-375-50388-9
1. Day trading (Securities)   2. Anuff, Joey.   3. Stockbrokers.
I. Wolf, Gary, 1962–   . II. Title.
HG4515.95.A58 2000
332.64'0285—dc21   99-056973

Random House Web site address: www.atrandom.com

Printed in the United States of America on acid-free paper

24689753

FIRST EDITION

Book design by Carole Lowenstein

Our joys as winged dreams do fly;
Why then should sorrow last?
Since grief but aggravates the loss,
Grieve not for what is past.
—ANONYMOUS

AUTHORS' NOTE

Attentive readers will notice that, while written in the first person, this book has two authors. Though the day-trading experiences described herein belong to Joey Anuff, at least 50 percent of the solecisms, exaggerations, misjudgments, and errors of fact belong to his collaborator, Gary Wolf.

CONTENTS

INTRODUCTION

These are the years of opportunity. In the late-afternoon sunshine of the twentieth century, good fortune has beamed down obligingly on equity owners everywhere. Rarely have capital gains been so easy.

Some people had the good luck to be born in a tropical paradise before European conquest. Some had the luck to be born wealthy in an enlightened age. It was my destiny—the equivalent, in contemporary thinking, to genius—to reach adulthood at the beginning of the most phenomenal bull market ever known.

At least I know enough to be grateful. I have earned little, but I have been denied less. Among the beneficiaries of unearned wealth, I rank, if not first among equals, squarely in the middle of the graduating class.

This is my story.

It is not a story about Wall Street. The image of a street is an inaccurate metaphor for where my form of "wealth creation" takes place. Wall Street, from its earliest days, was a kind of a club, with membership regulated by an evolving administration of gentlemen devoted to monopolizing the easy money. In exchange for guaranteed wealth, they undertook to bring order to the market.

With the help of the government, they succeeded. Since the Roosevelt administration, regular crashes and depressions have been tamed by close collaboration between Washington and Manhattan. This alliance has blessed us with deposit insurance, the Federal Reserve Bank, and the Securities and Exchange Commission. It gave us a set of dull and restrictive laws that enforced separation between the insurance industry, retail banking, and speculation in the financial markets. It gave us mutual funds, prosperity, and a stable postwar system.

And that, my friend, is the last of you'll hear of any of those virtues from me.

Many years ago, the New York Stock Exchange attempted to lure crash-wary small investors into the market with a patriotic campaign. "Own your share of America" was the slogan. "There is no stock exchange in Moscow," added G. Keith Funston, the president of the Exchange, "nor is ownership of promising enterprises in Russia available to the public." Funston's hope was that democracy would be safer in the hands of people who had pride of ownership in capitalist enterprise. This was the altruistic motive. The pecuniary motive was expressed by fixed trading fees of as high as 12 percent.

This situation has evolved somewhat in recent decades. For one thing, trading costs have plummeted. Also, nobody needs to be reassured anymore about the moral legitimacy of stock ownership. Patriotism, having served its purpose, no longer intrudes. It is just as well. In my view, which I take to be the majority opinion, the only reason to own your share of American enterprise today is to sell that share to somebody who is just a little bit more eager than you to bet on its future.

To understand what I have to say about day trading, it is important to get into the right frame of mind. When you think of stocks, do visions of companies and products float into your head? Does Nike mean running shoes? Does McDonald's mean hamburgers? Does Microsoft mean software?

You must break that habit. Purge these associations from your memory banks.

It won't be easy. The day-trading environment is designed to confuse. That interview with the beefy, shifty-eyed metals-industry executive on CNBC suggests that there are people and products behind the symbol on your desktop, that somewhere in the tropical heat bare-chested ex-farmers are digging metal deposits out of ex-forests. This may in fact be the case, but it has nothing to do with you. The chart of the mining company's stock, if extended back far enough, tells a complicated story of its long-term relationship with its workers, its customers, and its investors. But remember—you are not a worker or a customer. Unless things go very wrong, you are not an investor, either. Nothing causes day traders more amusement than evidence of a core group of believers *married* to the stocks they buy. By married I mean they keep their shares through thick and thin, in sickness and in health, for richer and for poorer.

To follow this story, you will have to gain mastery over your common sense, and learn to scorn the reality you are conditioned to think controls stock prices. You must not fear delusion and mania. As one well-known hedge-fund trader wrote recently, "The toughest thing in the world is to not blow out of an overvalued stock that is up 10. That is the definition of discipline in this market."

Finally, if you want to experience the glories of the new stock market, even vicariously, you need to have its main rule inscribed not just in your brain but in your stone-cold heart. Here is the rule: You are not an owner. You are not an investor. You are not an employee, customer, or stakeholder. You are not a patriotic American waving the flag, glad to go long in the name of freedom. *You are only in it for the money.*

There have always been pip-squeak brokerage customers who hustled for an inside line on a sure thing, or plunged their entire account plus margin on a tip about tomorrow's news. But the bull run on the Internet has produced an obsession with speculation that has no equal since Joseph Kennedy noticed in 1929 that the shoeshine boys were offering him market advice. All across America, people of limited means and intelligence have gotten rich buying and selling companies like Yahoo and eBay and Amazon.

We live in an era of unprecedented opportunity for un-earned riches, and nobody can ignore the fact that if they don't grab for the gold ring now, the merry-go-round might jerk to a stop before they get another chance. It is already possible to look back with devastating hindsight. "If I'd only put ten thousand into America Online stock when I first opened my account," goes the internal dia-tribe, "I'd *already* be a millionaire."

Thousands of unremarkable people have already be-come ultrarich. Last year I finally woke up to the Big Question.

Why not me?

DUMB MONEY

CHAPTER ONE

VISUALIZE MONEY

Dawn—4:50 A.M. Pacific Standard Time

I am in bed, but I'm not sleeping.

Things could be worse. I could be long.

There was a time when I would hold a position overnight, but I found it destroyed even the distant dream of shut-eye. Mornings are bad enough without wondering if I'm going to start the day screaming obscenities at my computer screen as the shorts go bonkers dumping some scandalous POS I was stuck with at yesterday's close. POS is one of the many acronyms that have come to pepper my speech in the year since I became a day trader. An IPO, for instance, is an initial public offering of stock, perhaps in an Internet company with dwindling cash reserves and no profits. SEC stands for the Securities and Exchange Commission, a federal agency that does various things that remain obscure to me but that often figures in the stories of stocks I am following. POS is an acronym used with dismaying frequency on the Silicon Investor message boards by a stock guru named Anthony Elgindy, whom you will meet in a few hours—under less than ideal circumstances. POS refers to many of the stocks I make money on. Since this story is governed by the rules of full disclosure, I have to admit that POS stands for "piece of shit."

My problem this morning is that without a position to worry me, I have trouble becoming alert. Every day I wake to the voices of CNBC, set to come on automatically at ten minutes before five A.M. And every day I have my first mini-panic right then, at the moment the lucidity of my predawn dream is replaced by the calmly alternating voices of Mark Haines and Maria Bartiromo, who seem like they've been talking to each other forever.

"Wait," I say to myself, still too groggy for an exclamation mark but troubled all the same, "how long has the TV been on? Have I missed the open? Did I oversleep?" And it takes all the effort in the world to turn my head and look for a quote from the red numbers on my digital clock. It says 4:50:06. The TV has been on for six seconds. I have won my first victory over the numbers.

Attentiveness slowly builds from there. Lying in bed, I notice a sensation that is halfway between Christmas morning and the day of your first sphincterotomy, a creeping sensation not of alertness but of anticipation and anxiety. I couldn't go back to dreamland if I wanted to. But I'm far from awake enough to make split-second financial decisions that will make me rich or ruin my life. In ten minutes or so, premarket trading will begin, and between now and then I have to remember how to cogitate.

If I were long overnight, thinking would be easier, but more painful. When I was an innocent new speculator, ten months ago, I would go to sleep with positions open, and my first thoughts of the day would be of multiplication tables. In the seventeen and a half hours between market close and the next day's open, revolutions in perception are commonplace, especially in the volatile low-cap stocks where I've made my biggest money. All night long, the amateur traders battle on the Internet message boards, insulting each other and trying to pump the price up or down, depending on whether they are long or short. When I held my positions, I was motivated to follow the battle as it dragged on for days, and I would spring up each morning, eager to learn how fate had treated me. Instead of doing jumping jacks, I got revved by multiplying 1500 shares of YHOO by 2, 4, or 5⅞ dollars.

But in the year gone by, I have grown up and put away childish things. These days, if I need to tabulate my folly I simply refer to the handy promotional mouse pad I got from a day-trading brokerage. The gimme pad features a grid showing the gains or losses on trades of 200, 500, 600, 800, 1000, 1500, and 2000 shares on stocks that move in ¹⁄₃₂ increments. No need to work excessively hard: here is the subtotal at a glance.

And anyway, I no longer need to calculate subtotals in the morning, because in the fall of 1998 I became a day trader, not in the loose, vernacular sense of the phrase—

encompassing as it does everyone from the casual Yahoo investor to the sixteenth-point penny-stock scalper—but in the true, volume-trading, ending-the-day-in-cash sense. When I became a day trader, I made it my rule not to hold positions overnight. Therefore, I no longer get up each morning to the possibility of a miracle or a disaster. The downside is that this makes it a lot harder to bring the world into focus. I have to get going from a dead stop. No profits, no losses to prick the brain.

It is now five A.M., and I put on a pot of coffee, though I know it won't work. Next I turn on my monitors. The computer whirs all night, but that's okay; to me it sounds like the ocean. I reboot the system and turn my modem off and on again, flushing out any voodoo irregularities that may have built up. I do the same for my digestive system, munching a cold, cinnamon-flavored frosted Pop Tart.

Coffee is preposterously overrated as a stimulant, although it does have other, healthful effects. The masterful Martin "Buzzy" Schwartz, who promoted himself as "Wall Street's Champion Trader," pointed out in his piquant autobiography how important it is to take laxative precautions in the hours before trading, as an unwelcome bathroom break can be damaging to your net worth. Thank God, coffee still has the needed effect.

After the third cup of coffee comes the high point of my morning (up to the point I make money). I open the friendly white box and chew a tab of Nicorette. I marvel at how many ashtrays I'd need if I were trading as a smoker. Good traders are supposed to be bloodless machines, according to the stereotype, but my Nicorette gives me a feeling of sensual, reflective pleasure as profound as any experienced by poets or mountain climbers; plus, I can make money at the same time.

Finally, it's time to get busy. I open a chat window or two, logging in to various real-time day-trading discussion rooms: free ones with names like *daytraders* and *bastages,* and some I've paid for, like *mtrader* and *mtclass.* At best, I'll find the time to follow one of them, but if I don't have all of them open, all through the trading day, I tend to get stress headaches. I bust open an Internet Explorer window to briefing.com, enjoying a special thrill if I've done so before they release the first of what will ultimately be fifty or so 150-word bulletins on trading stocks. And then I pull up the quotes.

Unfortunately—maybe it was the Nicorette—now I'm *too* relaxed. The day is dawning lavender and pink over Mount Diablo in the east, and with the FDA-approved two-milligram dose of orally administered nicotine coursing through my veins, it feels good simply to be alive, even if I haven't made a million dollars yet and here I am almost thirty. I am tempted to cut class. What would happen if I bashed my bare heel through this whirring, whining bank of monitors and went out for a stroll in the brightening city?

This is a mental trap I've learned to recognize and avoid. There will be plenty of time for enlightenment later, after I've banged the market up and down and retired on the tax-free municipal bonds I plan to purchase with my profits. The key to getting rich is wanting to be rich. And the key to wanting to be rich is not meditating on everyday beauty but thinking about other people—especially people you don't like—who are already rich. Success in this business is all about motivation, and although this book is not a training manual, I would like to share with you the special process I use when my attention wanders. Other successful traders hold weekend seminars and charge thousands of dollars for secrets of this sort. I don't need that extra cash. Here's my technique, revealed for free.

First, I close my eyes for a moment and imagine myself rising out of my body, through the twenty-four-foot ceiling of my loft and into the skies above my neighborhood, which is south of Market Street in San Francisco, near the foot of the Bay Bridge. To the east, facing commuters driving into the city, is a neon billboard announcing the week's Lotto jackpot. The prize this morning is three and half million dollars. I rise above the sign and look down upon the new construction. Auto shops and printing businesses are being replaced with two-story structures that look like the shells of racquetball courts but are really the wooden frames of one-room, $600,000 live-work condominiums. Waiting to buy the new homes are people I've worked with in the Internet industry for the past five years, every one of them more successful than me. I imagine my Internet colleagues looking up at the lottery sign and laughing with warm condescension at its puny payoff. One of them repeats a statistical factoid for my benefit. "You are less likely to win the lottery than you are to die from an infection by flesh-eating bacteria," he chuckles, winningly.

I think back on the time I had lunch with Jeff Bezos, the founder of Amazon.com, the year after he founded his company. We were sitting together at an outdoor buffet during a dull technology conference, and I suddenly considered asking him for a job. After all, I read books. Perhaps I should renounce my labors at an Internet start-up and join the quiet side of the industry. Go write reviews or something. But I was too busy with the dessert plate to give this serious thought. We finished our petits fours, shook hands, and parted. That skinny, balding guy in the open-collared white shirt with a bit of cream from an éclair leaking out of the corner of his mouth is a multibillionaire now, I remind myself. Then I think of a person I once interviewed for a job, and turned down, who went over to Netscape to write press releases six months before their initial public offering. He currently lives in Hawaii, where he is learning guitar.

Finally, I drift west, over the Mission District, and stare at a billboard that carries a giant advertisement for SportsLine.com, an online sports information network. Tiger Woods, many times larger than life, stands beside two slogans. The first says "Expect Greatness." Slightly below, there is an even more inspirational tag line: "NASDAQ: SPLN." SPLN is SportsLine's stock symbol. It is on the billboard to remind people that while they may never play a game of golf with Tiger Woods, they can still get a piece of the action. And not merely by visiting the SportsLine site—that's almost beside the point. What SportsLine is really advertising is the opportunity to purchase one or many shares of the company's stock.

The billboard works. Somebody made big money off of that tip. And that somebody wasn't me.

I feel my concentration sharpening. By the time the market opens, I might even be ready to trade.

Like other day traders, I am interested in stocks that move. I don't care if they stay up when they go up, because I'll take my profits at the first hint of a downturn (or, if I'm short-selling, at the first hint of an uptick). But the bull market is important to me all the same. The average investors—my victims—are natural longs. People of average and below-average intelligence won't plunge into a stock unless there is clear evidence that prices are going up. Slow, careful accumulation by cautious mutual fund managers doesn't make any stock quadruple in value over a few weeks. For that kind of action, you need Mr. Smith to come home from work with a little brain fatigue and sit down in front of the television set and hear for the millionth time that the Dow has broken through to a new high, and that the leading gainer for the day is one or another little-known Internet stock that does something earthshaking, like selling dental floss over the Web. Eventually, all the Mr. Smiths will pile in. My goal is to beat them by at least a few seconds.

But it's not just Mr. Smith I'm playing against. There

are also all my fellow day traders, who are themselves trying to get on the bus ahead of Mr. Smith. I have to beat
them, too. And when lots and lots of us have piled in, and
the stock has shot up, and the dumb-money interest has
waned, I've got to jump off quickly, before the damn bus
slows down to less than fifty miles per hour and explodes.
I'm not really worried about jumping off ahead of Mr.
Smith. He'll leap, eventually, but not until he's lost a sub-
stantial amount of his money. Smith's great virtue is that
he is willing to suffer losses. (Thank you, thank you, and
thank you again, Smith!) But the day traders—they're a
different story. They will fake me out and push me aside
and, if necessary, run me over in their race to beat me off
the bus. As I would them.

Day traders are very competitive. But beside our mutual desire to screw each other is another sentiment we
share: regret. Regret is the day trader's most intensely felt
emotion. It is the key to his or her personality. What lust
is to Don Giovanni; what rage is to Rambo; slack-jawed,
head-shaking disappointment is to the men and women
who make their living via the sale and purchase of listed
stocks. I've been around lots of traders, and I know that
the only thing they like better than bragging about their
profits is mourning the profits they didn't make.

It is truly maddening to miss a great bull run. *It would
have been so easy,* you tell yourself. Or maybe you try to
comfort yourself with the idea that a Wall Street tycoon is
as distant and untouchable as a Hollywood star. Both fit
comfortably on the cover of *Vanity Fair* and have homes

designed to impress the editors of *Architectural Digest*. Millions dream of kissing the face of one and the ass of the other. Yet they are not the same. The wealthiest names of Wall Street—the Warren Buffetts and Peter Lynches and George Soroses—were not born with pretty faces or beautiful voices or even gargantuan superbrains. They simply started small and bet well, and got good seats on the best buses. And just think, you were standing right next to them on the curb! What's your excuse for not sipping wine with them in your Gulfstream IV right now? You don't have one. Regrets: that's all you have.

So fabulous are the market's hypothetical rewards that even the missed opportunities of other traders bring you down. Day traders often appropriate each other's celebrated blunders and castigate themselves for not having gotten in on somebody else's great deal. David Wetherell, the chairman of the Internet incubator fund CMGI, has said that his biggest mistake, one that took him years to overcome, was passing on an early investment in eBay. Every time eBay runs up another 30 percent, I join in his remorse, berating myself for not having put a few dollars into the company back in 1996—even though I didn't have a few dollars in 1996.

In 1994, Microsoft cofounder Paul Allen sold a 25 percent stake in AOL at a split-adjusted price of less than a buck a share, missing out on approximately ten billion dollars in profits. I cringe in embarrassment—I didn't have faith in AOL then, either. If only I'd put $10,000 in AOL in 1994, it'd have turned into a million a year ago.

On the other hand, in 1994 I was still being tossed off AOL for sending around pirated copies of Doom. Embracing the corporation as a long-term investor was low on my five-year plan. Nonetheless, my failure pains me deeply.

A few years back, a reporter asked Bill Gates what type of Internet company he thought would be successful. Gates answered, "All of them." Anyone who'd taken him seriously would be seriously rich now. The wild flight paths of the most famous stocks play games with the imagination. The very bets that seemed the most foolish in 1998 provided the greatest gains of 1999. You could've bought $10,000 of Yahoo when every expert was laughing at its sky-high valuation, and seen your pittance turn into well over $100,000 before a year was over. The same plunge in E*Trade would have produced a $150,000 windfall. In fact, you could've bought just about any Internet stock in August of 1998, when the bloom appeared to be off the rose, and by thumbing your nose at common sense you would have "earned" 1,000 percent in less time than it takes to manufacture an infant.

Many contemplate what it would have meant for them had they pulled this off, but it goes without saying that almost nobody did. It's a lot easier to check a stock's fifty-two-week high and low at finance.yahoo.com than it is to buy YHOO at the low and sell it at the high. The seductive fantasy of maximum gains keeps millions nibbling at the market—and contributing to momentum when a run begins.

For the day trader, humble pie is a regular diet. Why

didn't I buy Netbank last month when it was getting play on the Yahoo message boards? Why didn't I buy TCI Music a few weeks ago when the first rumors of the Liberty Media acquisition started goosing its price upwards? Why didn't I buy Schwab two days ago when it started running in advance of today's split?

Can you grasp the agony? This isn't about not buying Microsoft stock back when I was twelve years old. It isn't about failing to invest in eBay back when I was filling out résumés at Starbucks. And it isn't about failing to keep my AOL investment back when I was Paul Allen. This *really* almost happened. I had an account. I was paying attention. I had my finger ready. True humiliation is knowing that you missed a chance at effortless riches not a year or a month or a day ago but *five seconds* ago. Hindsight, they say, is always twenty-twenty. To be a day trader is to watch the unknowable future pass into the obvious present every second. To be a day trader is to make regret into a lifestyle.

Each day, in the hours before the market opens, a thick layer of bullshit spreads across the trading community. Well, you call it bullshit. I call it *fertilizer.* My job is to sift through the muck and guess where the beautiful flowers will pop up.

Earnings reports from yesterday afternoon are reexamined. *Is it good that Amgen beat the First Call earnings estimate, or bad that it missed its whisper numbers?* Press releases tell of partnerships, great-big plans, and unexpected windfalls. *Emusic.com got mentioned in* Barron's! Acquisition rumors worm their way from telephone to message boards to TV screens, 100 percent true until denied. *If Bell Atlantic doesn't actually merge with Vodaphone it'll be a shame; they should!* Stock splits are announced that would be meaningless but for the widespread belief that somewhere in Iowa there's a dentist who thinks a split will make the price go up. This becomes a self-fulfilling prophecy as thousands of day traders scramble to beat the dentist. *Shares of Harmonic Inc. and Conexant bid up 8 ½ and 2 points respectively on two-for-one split news!* Analyst recommendations—invariably upgrades, invariably on companies the analysts' firms took public exactly thirty days ago—hit the digital airwaves. *DLJ starts coverage of recent IPO Wink Communications with "buy!" Merrill Lynch starts recent IPO Netro Corp with "buy!" Hambrecht and Quist starts recent IPO Novamed Eyecare with, hold on a second . . . yes, with "buy!"*

Below it all runs the S&P futures, which foretell whether all or any of the above will live to see market close. Today, the S&Ps put everybody in positive territory. It's going to be a pleasant day.

If it were Friday morning, I'd have more fun stocks to watch. On Thursday evening, traders start pondering the immediate growth potential of at least three stocks: the picks for next week's "Inside Wall Street" column in *Business Week.* A little while back, one of them sounded good to me: SPGLA, the symbol for *Der Spiegel,* or maybe just

Spiegel, I can't recall. The story had something to do with the immediate acquisition potential of the media powerhouse, which is either a catalog or a magazine. It didn't really matter. The stock was at eight bucks and "Inside Wall Street" thought it could be worth twenty in a takeover. Although takeover targets mentioned in "Inside Wall Street" never actually get acquired, I saw some nibbling on my Level II screen. I bought. Before the market opened Friday, I sold it all for a handsome profit. By Monday, it was back below Thursday's close.

Unfortunately, it's not Friday. Which means I'll have to search just a little harder for today's hot air balloons.

I'm not too concerned; there's sure to be something juicy; and now market is about to open and start calling me on my bullshit in real time.

CHAPTER TWO

THE
DAILY GRIND

Imagine the contrast between a stock exchange and the day-trader's workstation. The chaos on the trading floor versus the quiet in my money-minting loft space; the physical intensity of the New York Stock Exchange specialists as they fill bids and asks versus the relaxed but ergonomically erect posture encouraged by my $800 Herman Miller chair; the raspy voice and tired arches of the man on the floor versus the reserves of energy I've stored up by declining to pursue any difficult or socially useful labor. Recently I was in the offices of Black Rocket, the advertising agency for Discover Brokerage. Discover is the online trading firm owned by Morgan Stanley Dean Witter. One of the Black Rocket advertisements shows an angelic child whose face is awash in the glow of a computer screen. The caption says: "We've made investing so easy even a child can do it. Perhaps we've gone too far." I am that child, beating the market up and down from the peace of my crib.

There might actually be a little bit more peace if I turned the TV down, but it is rumored that sometime after the open there will be a CNBC mention of the proposed Bell Atlantic acquisition of Vodaphone. I don't want to get distracted and miss it, so the room is echoing with the sound of CNBC's *Countdown to Market Open.* A dull roar of excited voices ricochets off my walls and ceiling, competing with the CNBC theme song, which I find myself whistling absentmindedly in taxis and on elevators. (You'd be shocked to know how many times a taxi driver or elevator rider has suddenly started whistling along.) Then comes the ceremonial open, when the honored guest of the day strikes the opening bell. He is raising his arm. And . . .

Ding! Ding! Ding! The market is up at the open and it's Pamplona around here and I'm running as fast as my typing fingers can carry me to stay ahead of the bulls. I've been told that the best day traders are former Air Force pilots and ex–college athletes and others who have practice staying calm under pressure, but I devour ghost-written bios of Wall Street giants like M&Ms, hoping to pick up trading clues and new slang, and I can tell you, based on *volumes* of secondhand knowledge, that traders do not stay calm on days when the market is jumping around like crazy. My mouth is hanging open and my eyes are practically rolling around in my head, but somehow I am able to absorb information from the windows open on my three monitors, each of which is showing an impressive amount of disorder. Prices on volatile Internet stocks are jumping ten whole points as the market tries to figure out whether it is going up or down. I'm tracking six stocks in detail—all bids, asks, and executions for these six are lined up atop a real-time chart that shows prices going back minute by minute to the open of the market. I have another forty stocks updating in a table that shows me the prints (actual sales) and other essential information.

Every one of my Big Six is trading in what the authorities call a "fast market," where bids and asks are flying so fast they can't be efficiently matched. Five minutes ago RBAK was down 2 bucks; now it is either up 4 or up 8, depending on which numbers I believe. The flicker of digits in the columns and the terse acronyms—*sld msft 90¼; bot 87*—scrolling by the traders' chat rooms that I monitor contain as much coded hope and delusion as the dates and initials inscribed on the inside of a wedding band, despite the fact that the relationship in question won't outlast the hour.

Once, when I explained what I was doing for money, a friend asked, "Isn't it boring, sitting in front of a computer screen all day?" Of course not, I told her. It's never boring making money. And it isn't only the money. I stepped up to the trading screen from a childhood of Asteroids and Pac-Man and Doom, where little graphical symbols convincingly represented missile fire and cannibalism and mass murder. This is the same thing, only more violent.

What am I looking for? What I want is a story stock, a gainer that cracks through layers of resistance like a rocket on its way to the moon. Sometimes you can sense the potential energy in a stock for weeks. Say there's a laggard in an industry where all the major players have already been hyped up to three or four times their fifty-two-week low. Something is holding the runt of the litter back—maybe the company president was scapegoated for misreported earnings, or a vaunted partnership with a bigger firm has hit the skids, or the corporation in question has just arrived on the scene, jettisoning its former identity as a dry-cleaning-supplies wholesaler and only recently reconstituting itself as an online travel agency. Investors are wary.

This is the sign of opportunity. Sooner or later, the board of directors and the executives, who own millions of shares of this low-volume, two-dollar stock, are going to find themselves a pleasant-voiced president, or scare up a new partnership, or float a press release touting a successful first quarter of online reservation booking. This wisp of news, when it hits the news wires that flash press releases on traders' screens, will cause a sudden blip in the price, and if all goes well and the movement is noted by the active traders who share tips and rumors on the stock-trading boards, the price will blip again, which will earn it a place on the big-gainer lists, which will cause it to blip again, and then—maybe, maybe—Joe Kernen will give it fifteen seconds of attention on CNBC, and then it's time to sell, because we have our home run for the day. And even if I don't get all the way around the bases, I'll take my double, with pleasure. In reality, the stocks I covet tend to be no-name companies offering bluntly underwhelming newsflashes, but as long as they function as stand-ins for the corporate miracle of the moment, they'll do.

One morning not long ago I had my eye on three candidates, all with wonderful nonsense names that I hoped would provide the necessary whiff of the incomprehensible that connotes the high-tech future. The first was iTurf (TURF), a "Gen Y" community site that was going steadily downhill. ITurf's revenues beat analysts' expectations by a few cents, though this year's numbers were behind last year's. The second prospect was Liquid Audio (LQID), a software company that offers a music distribution scheme over the Internet. I don't know anybody who uses Liquid Audio, but they have just announced the release of their new software suite. The third possible winner was Network Event Theater (NETS), a multiservice portal for college students. Network Event Theater had just acquired an obscure college-student site, Collegeweb.com, perhaps because they wanted to use the URL.

The sign that a stock has started to catch the interest of the crowd is an increase in the number of trades. The stock market is often compared to a Las Vegas casino, but this is inaccurate. It is more like the pari-mutuel system at the track, since you are taking money from other players rather than from the house. Money is harder to come by on a rainy, sparsely attended weekday at Belmont, when only the rabid fans and the professionals are in attendance. You want a lot of Sunday race-goers willing to drop fifty bucks on a horse because its name sounds like their daughter's pretty gym teacher. So it is with online trading: the more little traders who are moving in and out of a stock, the better the chance that I'm not the biggest fool in the game, and that somebody will still be getting on the bus when I'm ready to get off it. TURF and NETS were rising, but on low volume. On this particular morning, they knew no love.

Liquid Audio, on the other hand, was being fêted as the crown prince of the music revolution. On the day they went public, their stock shot up to almost 50 dollars a share. In the ensuing weeks it had dropped below 18, punishing the gullible severely. Lately it had been bouncing around in the mid-30s. I tried not to question why the long-expected release of a software product by a company that has been steadily sinking since its first day on the market would cause the price to suddenly shoot up. Who knows why? Perhaps it provided conclusive evidence that the company still existed.

I used to bother myself with silly questions about the *real reason* a stock rose. I was disturbed, for instance, by the way a stock would run in advance of a split. A split cuts the share price in half and doubles the numbers of shares. This should make absolutely no difference to anybody. But a volatile stock will almost always run up for a few days before the split, and then sell off when people take profits. It is as mysterious as the movement of ants or bees, and as predictable. I came to the conclusion that a split worked like nuclear fission: a little split produced a lot of energy.

Not long after the bell, LQID was at 28⅜, up almost three points from yesterday's close. That's the kind of pace I like. Some investors will satisfy themselves with 10 percent a year—but LQID was offering better than 10 percent *an hour.* I also liked the volume. If Liquid Audio had seen as many copies of their software downloaded as shares traded before open, it might actually have been worth what people were paying.

A few minutes later LQID cooled down a bit, with the overnight holders and premarket buyers taking their profits. It moved down a buck or so, and just when the selling stopped and before a new wave of buyers came in, I took my shot and snagged 500 shares at 28¼. By watching your screen carefully, you can see the selling slow down. The movement falters and levels off. There are a handful of prints at 28⅜, then a print at 28⁵⁄₁₆, then another handful at 28¼, then another at 28⅜, then yet another at 28¼. If you have guts, you buy the stock now rather than waiting for it to start an obvious move upward. It's a beautiful feeling, being in at the bottom and gazing calmly as the stock wavers at a few ticks above what you paid for it—and then decides to rally. Buying before you see definite movement upward helps you keep your sanity when you face unforeseen circumstances such as I encountered moments after I made my trade. LQID failed to rally.

My stock edged up a few sixteenths, but no strong buying set in. There was no second wind. "Come on, you worthless blimp," I muttered. On top of my computer, I have taped a quote to remind me of the true nature of the stocks I'm playing. It is from a notorious pump-and-dump manipulator named Jerry Allen, whose newsletter, during the sixties, sang praises of companies that paid him a certain fee. To keep the boobs from thinking he was unnaturally optimistic, Allen would be extra realistic about the companies that neglected to pay him. "New issue soufflés," he once wrote, "are concocted by eggheads capitalizing on the public's demand for puffy stocks." Thirty years later, we still don't know any better. Somehow, on the morning in question, I ended up with $14,000 worth of just-out-of-the-oven Liquid Audio in my portfolio, and it looked like the air might be about to seep out. Luckily, I was still in the money.

All the mainstream investment experts insist that patience is the key to stock market success. After an eternity that lasted ten minutes, my patience finally paid off: briefing.com, a key source of constantly updated news headlines, mentioned the interest in LQID. A few minutes later CNBC's Joe Kernen noted in passing the increase in activity. And awaaaaay we go. LQID stock galloped up 3 dollars, breaking through 30. Step right up, suckers, there's plenty of room in the back. When the price touched 31⅜, I knew it was time to step off. I wanted out, but now there was a stampede. LQID was selling like mad. I had to get out of there. It hit 31¼. Come on you son of a bitch, sell! There were bids at 31 all down my screen, and one lone 31¼ at the top of the column. Fuck it. I'll take 31. I was still going to make $1,500 on a single trade. That's pretty good for one day, and it wasn't even seven A.M. yet.

But I didn't take 31. I was about to confirm my new sell order when the fleet little arrow on my monitor stopped moving in response to my mouse. My hands were banging on the keyboard, but nothing happened, and I heard in the distance something that sounded like a dozen cats in a sack being thrown off a bridge. It got louder and louder until I traced it to its source, which was my throat. By the time I rebooted my computer and signed back on, LQID was at 29, where I finally sold it. I lost most of my profits, but the pain ceased after the sale. A few seconds later, so did the screaming.

It was in the summer of 1999 that day trading finally produced a mass murderer—Mark O. Barton—and the only question was: What took so long? Everybody knew that testosterone-addled, foul-mouthed, money-blind stock speculators were ticking bombs. Barton walked out of the stereotype into reality when he marched into the office where he'd been trading and opened fire.

Weirdly, the only news outlet to unashamedly trumpet the day-trading angle was Rupert Murdoch's *New York Post,* where Barton was known as the Slay Trader. Elsewhere, the proximate cause of Barton's spree was quickly smoothed over. Harvey Houtkin, chairman and chief executive officer of All-Tech Investment Group, where Barton traded, doubted the shootings had "anything to do with a down day in the market." Mayor Bill Campbell of

Atlanta confessed to the press that "I don't know if we'll ever know what the true motives were." CNN headline-writers were especially perplexed. "Shooter lost $105,000 in month," they wrote, "but motive still a mystery."

All the news outlets were eager to point out that the mysterious hatchet murders of Barton's ex-wife and her mother in 1994, for which Barton was a suspect, suggested that he may have lost his marbles years before he took a wrong position in MP3.com or shorted eBay. Nonetheless, to those of us unburdened by the weighty responsibilities of the fourth estate, Barton was the obvious poster boy for market mania. The story of Barton was a believable cautionary tale to day traders—who live every second on the edge of panic—while doubling as a narrative of karmic retribution for those few Americans who still scorn trading.

We're lucky that most people never act on their feelings, because there's no denying that the stresses of day trading make many people feel like pulling the trigger. This was especially so in the summer of 1999. The impersonal traffic delays that spawn road rage are nothing compared to the merciless punishment available in the stock market on a bad morning, and for many day traders, most of the mornings since April had been bad. In the late spring and summer, the technology and Internet stocks beloved by Barton and other amateurs lost as much as half their value. What once seemed so easy—get up, buy YHOO, wait a few hours, sell YHOO, tally profits—became an anxiety-ridden nightmare of less-than-perfect timing.

The day-trading favorites didn't just go south, they went nutty. Good news was followed by sell-offs. Bad news caused unexpected runs. Once, in July, in the middle of the trading day, Amazon's Web site went down and customers were greeted with a message apologizing for technical difficulties. Instantly, the word spread across trading chat rooms and Internet message boards. Just as the little guys jumped into the action, the stock jerked upwards, wrecking those who had sold short on margin. Five minutes later, Amazon's Web site came back, good as new. The day traders not yet reduced to tears began buying in anticipation of a further rise. Naturally, the stock jerked downward again. This kind of thing provokes howls of pain on the message boards, inspires countless conspiracy theories, and produces a look of tight-lipped mayhem that ought to be known, if it isn't already, as trade rage.

Barton's last trade came just as the market turned, in April, so maybe he was whipsawed out of his trading account when the bull took a breather. Or maybe he just had a bad trade or two, not enough to wipe him out but enough to leave him afraid. Afraid he'd lost his touch; afraid his next trade would be another bankroll-burning blunder; afraid he was born to lose. It turned out to be much worse than we imagined, of course. Barton had day-traded away hundreds of thousands of dollars in life insurance he'd received after the death of his first wife. Then, he'd turned around and borrowed and lost another fortune that had been put away for his kids.

Experts insist that support from one's family is crucial

to a day-trading lifestyle. Without this support, every foolish trade carries a double price: not only do you lose your money, but you have to *admit* you lost your money. Barton's second wife had kicked him out of the house. He was broke, alone, bitter, and delusional. Had they known the situation, Barton's trading comrades would surely have preferred to be left alone in a room with a suitcase nuke.

"He didn't come to my firm first," said All-Tech's Houtkin, whom I asked about Barton a few months after the shooting. "He went first to Momentum, killed five or six people there, walked across the parking lot, composed himself, reloaded his weapons, walked into my firm, and greeted everybody. He even bought one trader a soda. The reason Mark Barton scared everybody so much was that he wasn't a loony, some Nazi who shoots up a community center. They considered him a friend."

Since gun-loving men with self-esteem problems provide the candidate pool from which Barton-style mass murderers are selected, it's downright terrifying to think of the trickle-down effect of the day-trading mania on all of us. After all, the stock market doesn't beat around the bush. It doesn't give A's for effort. It doesn't say, "Everybody is special, just in their own way." The stock market offers direct, quantitative confirmation of exactly how much of a loser you are. And at the moment you realize you are broke, other traders—those Barton referred to as "the greedy ones"—will be doing Cuba Gooding, Jr.–style victory dances around their computers, reminding you that your savings didn't merely vanish into thin air, they vanished into somebody else's trading account.

As the screams of my LQID losses died away, I found myself wondering whether the rush to absolve day trading of any responsibility for Barton's crimes didn't have some ulterior motives behind it. Could it be that the top journalists, whose retirement accounts are socked away in mutual funds, intuitively understood that a link between mass murder and the stock market might not be the best thing for the composite index?

On the other hand, maybe this self-censorship was short-sighted. It takes both positive and negative reinforcement to keep the bull moving, and having inflated the bubble for years with stories of little old ladies getting rich off their capital gains, it is probably time for another approach to delaying the pop. The smart thing would be to remind the nervous Nellies that there are other Bartons out there, in the silence, and that they are counting on the stock market to float them out of their misery. Yes, there are other Bartons out there, and they have a message for Mr. and Mrs. Small Investor.

The message is: "Keep buying stocks, or we'll kill you."

Maybe Barton should have known better. In the twelve months before he dumped his bank account into All-Tech Investment Group's convenient life-savings Porta Potti, the press was full of advice for would-be investors in the stock market. Unfortunately, in a raging bull market cautionary advice often has a different effect than intended.

Writing thirty years ago, during the extended bull run of
the go-go sixties, journalist Murrey Teigh Bloom chroni-
cled Jerry Allen's pump-and-dump career, and Bloom ex-
pertly dissected the psychology of the small-time plunger
victimized by stock newsletters, telephone tips, and brokers. "The sucker is often encouraged to speculate by all
these warnings about rising stock prices," he noted.
"They serve as a harsh reminder to him that others are
growing filthy rich in the market; and the sucker mentality, being what it is, construes the warnings as a sign that
'insiders' want to keep him out of a good thing."

Laughable? Maybe. But on the other hand, it is undeniable that the best times to get rich quick in the past few
years have been when respectable analysts were most
pessimistic about stocks—especially Internet stocks. How
does the non-sucker explain the strange but undeniable
fact that while he or she was listening to the presumably
well-meant warnings of the anti-speculators, a number of
idiots who were too stupid to know better were calling
their attorneys to set up tax dodges to protect their gigantic short-term capital gains.

All I have to do is look around my loft to see the price
I've paid for my lemminglike rush into these overvalued
new-issue soufflés. The car in my garage—that was uBid.
My living room set with couch and armchair—that was
E*Trade. And the walls and ceiling and floor, the doors
and bathroom and metal-hinged windows of the absurd
one-room apartment for which I pay an absurdly inflated
rent every month—all these delights I owe to a single

beautiful stock about which one astute commentator re-marked, in the fall of 1998, "What chance is there that a year from now we won't even remember that this com-pany exists?"*

EBay, I *worship* you.

EBay started the bull run in online auctions by en-abling secondhand sales of Beanie Babies. Tiny, furry toys with cute names, Beanie Babies were and are manufac-tured by Ty Inc., which cleverly limited the supply of any particular creature. Ostensibly aimed at children, Beanie Babies were quickly recognized by collectors as a nearly perfect analog for the stock market, and they began to speculate in Beanie Babies. There were Beanie Baby clubs, Beanie Baby newsletters, Beanie Baby analysts, and, in the end, a Beanie Baby bubble. At first, there was no equivalent to the New York Stock Exchange for Beanie Babies. Then the collectors discovered eBay.

EBay was tailor-made for speculation in children's toys. The company began as a Web site that Pierre Omid-yar created to support his girlfriend's interest in buying and trading Pez dispensers. Before long, the site had a fa-natical following of collectors of all kinds of rare and pseudo-rare objects. The exaggerated valuation accepted by buyers of the secondhand toys, comic books, and porcelain figurines was exceeded only by the exaggerated price placed on them by the sellers. Shortly before eBay

* James Surowiecki, "MoneyBox," on Slate, September 24, 1998.

went public in September 1998, bids for a Royal Blue Peanut the Elephant reached $2,850—but failed to meet the seller's minimum price. A friend of mine named Tim Cavanaugh tried to convince me that the Beanie Baby market was actually safer than the stock market. Tim took his theory public on my Web site, Suck.com. "In a market sustained by limitless belief," he wrote, "everything depends on your fellow zealots keeping the faith. With markets sustained by the Greater Fool Theory, you're better off in a market that's full of fools."

As the editor of Suck, however, I knew that Tim was just reaching for a punch line under the pressure of a deadline. The real money was not going to be made in Beanies. As I've already mentioned, it isn't just the relative stupidity of the average investor—in stocks or stuffed animals—that matters. Volume, or the total quantity of aggregated stupidity, is also very important. And however popular Kara the Kangaroo becomes, she will never win a popularity contest against a publicly traded corporation.

I had searched eBay many times since it launched, though not for Beanie Babies. My interests were more sophisticated: I was hoping to find a few issues to add to my collection of *Mad* magazines. When I first visited eBay in 1997, I found that the site had grown far beyond its base among Pez fans. It offered more than 400,000 items for sale. Every time anything is sold on eBay, the company's cut is 1.5 to 5 percent. Plus, sellers pay between a quarter and two dollars for each listing. Who cared if two out of ten or even three out ten users didn't pay up? The costs were fixed. The profits were infinite. EBay scaled. It was as if every entry on Yahoo had a for-sale sticker on it. It was as if Amazon had found a way to shut down their warehouse for good, fire 90 percent of their staff, and maintain their level of sales. Given that unprofitable Internet companies with no discernable business model were valued at billions of dollars, how much would a profitable Internet company with a great business model be worth? The answer was clear: zillions of dollars.

When eBay filed documents with the Securities and Exchange Commission in preparation for going public, outlining the details of their business, it became sickeningly obvious how much money was about to made. As the big day approached, the number of daily auctions reached almost a million. There was little chance of eBay opening at 18 dollars a share. Internet users loved it too much. As the August weeks passed, I lived each day in fear that everyone would realize what was as clear as day to me. EBay wouldn't only be the hot internet IPO of the year. EBay wouldn't just be a strong e-commerce player over the next few years. EBay *was* e-commerce.

Look close to home, wrote Peter Lynch, an old-style investment guru whose wisdom I'd come across in an attractive, easy-to-read anthology. Lynch recommended investing in pharmaceutical companies that make drugs for chronic illnesses. "A great patient's drug," he said, "is one that cures an affliction once and for all, but a great investor's drug is one that the patient has to keep buying."

But there is an even better type of drug. The best drugs

are the ones that soothe the symptoms while making the disease *worse.* The best drug doesn't just cure patients, it creates addicts. By the time eBay's IPO was announced, I was searching for about fifty things every day. EBay was what I did when I didn't have anything useful to do—which, since I had a full-time job in the Internet industry, was most of the time. EBay had become part of my unconscious procrastination routine.

I had traveled in an increasingly wide spiral away from my core interests. In addition to *Mad* magazines, I was searching for mint issues of *The New Yorker* from the twenties, *Esquires* from the sixties, Wacky Packages from the seventies, copies of *Spy* from the eighties. I checked every day for the appearance of a Steve Austin action figure, if only to remind myself that a mere twenty years ago people thought you could build a superman for only six million dollars. By the time I bid on a cheesy, plastic, flashing, muttering robot called ROM Spaceknight (still in the box)—which I had envied when I was seven years old—I knew that eBay was the killer app. I needed that robot. It was a bookmark from my childhood that marked the place of a deep narcissistic injury. With the help of Nicorette, I quit smoking. But I could never quit eBay.

Unfortunately, trying to get in on the eBay IPO was more difficult than finding an unopened toy robot from 1974. And it had a sneaky side effect. Since I wasn't a multimillionaire with a full-service account at the big banking house that was taking eBay public, I wasn't likely to get a personal invitation to invest. But E*Trade, the most aggressive of the online brokerage houses, was offering a special promotional deal to its users. Investors with an E*Trade account got access to a limited number of shares of new IPOs. Each investor could take a minimum of 100 shares. Or was it a maximum? The rules seemed purposefully unclear. I knew the subscription would be sold out almost instantly. To equalize the inconvenience and maximize the user's time on E*Trade—during which he or she might get bored and trade a few other stocks and generate some money in commissions—the IPO shares would become available at an unspecified time. You had to be online, and paying attention, when they came up for sale, or else you wouldn't get them. I watched the site nearly twenty-four hours a day for a month.

I sat on the page advertising the eBay IPO. And I clicked. And I sat some more. And I refreshed. I fiddled with Internet Explorer, trying to set it up to send me an instant update the minute the IPO page changed. It didn't work. And while I was fiddling some more, there it was. "E*Trade is now accepting indications of interest in the upcoming eBay IPO." First, I had to fill out an eligibility profile. How long had I been investing? *5–10 years,* I lied. What is your net worth? *$200K–$500K,* I lied. How many shares would I like? *3000, please.* A week or so later, I got 100. If I'd merely kept my $2,000 stake and not made any other moves, it would be worth well over $50,000 right now. But I wasn't at all satisfied with such a piddling plunge. After all, I knew it was a sure thing, and I was going to get into the market with everything I had.

I liquidated my mutual funds, and at six A.M. Pacific time on September 24, 1998, eBay shares became available to the eager public. The first trade was at 53, nearly three times the offering price by the underwriters. By the time I'd spent my savings on 900 additional shares, the price was already 54.

By the end of the following week, I had lost $5,000. The financial press was loving the story—eBay soared on the first day of trading and then immediately began to fall. Everybody was losing money except the insiders who bought at the offering price. The financial columnist at Slate piled on, making a few jokes at the expense of the "money-losing" auction site and its pathetic fans. "You dumbfucks," I screamed across the gridlocked blocks of San Francisco, over the horizon, toward Slate's offices in Redmond, Washington, "eBay isn't losing money! It's *making* money!"

This was my savings they were talking about here. I was well into my twenties, with no skills discernable to anyone outside the topsy-turvy Internet economy, where I was mysteriously deemed employable—and here were a bunch of self-righteous journalists messing with my one good shot at independent wealth, and getting the story wrong, besides. For months I'd been watching overvalued Internet companies make millionaires out of some of the most clueless people I knew. I'd finally convinced myself that in this market, advertent or inadvertent cluelessness was not only *not* a disadvantage, it was a prerequisite. Even the hardheaded Doug Henwood, a stick-in-the-mud socialist critic of the financial markets, had figured out the rules of the bull market. "Euphoric self-deception," he wrote in his book *Wall Street*, "makes new equity offerings possible."

The underwriters and executives of the new companies did everything but stick it in the documents they file with the Securities and Exchange Commission: "Purchasers of this stock must be capable of believing anything." And now, when I'd finally gotten with the program, eBay was acting terribly, terribly rationally. EBay was plummeting, and with every point it dropped, I lost $1,000.

Perhaps I was still being too reasonable. Maybe the problem was that eBay had a real business. Maybe they weren't "blue sky" enough. Amazon, after all, was still saying, "Remember, we're not in the book business." Not only was Amazon losing money, but you had to wait five more years before you found out what their business really was. This meant there was no way to figure out what the value was.

In contrast, eBay was making money. Maybe by the time you actually make money, all the fun is out of the stock. And yet, eBay had incredible business momentum. They were invulnerable to competition. You could always make another bookstore. How do you make another eBay? Sellers go where the buyers are, and buyers go where the sellers are, and almost all the sellers and buyers were on eBay. In ten years, who was going to be thriving—eBay, or Yahoo, whose price-to-earnings ratio stood at more than one thousand?

Microsoft had spent tens of millions on an ill-fated attempt to start locally oriented Web sites and get local classified advertising away from newspapers, and now eBay had won the war without employing so much as a single journalist. Who was going to be putting anything in a newspaper classified section now—where it cost you twenty bucks and you didn't even get a good price? On eBay, it cost less than a dollar, and you didn't get just buyers, you got bidders.

This was the lecture I gave, standing at my window and looking east toward the gray water of the bay as the grim morning advanced. Every few seconds I turned my head to see how much money I'd lost. Sometimes I leaned my hot face against the glass and tried to cry. Still, the stock fell. Down, down, down. I panicked and closed out my position while it was still in the 40s. I'd never lost so much money so fast in my life.

Like a rejected lover who hangs around outside his exgirlfriend's house until she gets a restraining order and he's hassled off the corner by the unsympathetic police, I couldn't take my eyes off eBay, though I was no longer a shareholder. I was convinced we were meant for each other. Someday, that stock was going to rally out of obscurity and become the darling of the Internet investor, and when it began to venture out again I wanted, more than anything else, a second chance.

I kept my E*Trade account, and in early October I took a long road trip with my girlfriend. Driving from Boston to Raleigh, I checked the price by phone every three hours.

EBay just kept dropping. One morning at a Kinko's in Washington, D.C., on a rented computer, I learned that eBay had opened at 32⅝ after closing at 30⅛ the night before. I'd vowed to reenter at 22, and now it looked like I'd never get my chance. The next day, Friday, it closed at 36. On Monday, it hit 46. I swallowed hard, and with the remaining total of my damaged savings and a few thousand from an inheritance from my father, I bought half my position back: 500 shares.

I really didn't have any choice, because if it rose past the point where I had sold it on the way down, I was going to have to kill myself. It was bad enough having been long and wrong. Now I risked being right and on the sidelines. I'd been yelling at my brother Ed for weeks about how eBay was going to be the stock of the century. If I didn't own any when it broke out, I'd be explaining for the rest of my life why I was still asking him to lend me money.

I was staying in Raleigh with some friends when the big bang came. Our holiday recreation program involved doing bong hits and watching NASCAR on ESPN2, and for some reason I felt paranoid about asking them to change the channel to CNBC. So when they would go outside to piss on a tree or paint pinstripes on their toilet seat, I would sneak a peek, hoping to catch Amanda Grove on the floor of the stock exchange saying what was happening to my company. I didn't really have to worry about tuning in at the right moment, because during these weeks they were *always* talking about eBay. It was going up 20 points a day. I would be sitting on the legless sofa, an upholstery spring poking into my butt cheek, choking on some homegrown and thinking, "I can't *believe* this. I just made ten thousand dollars!"

The incredible thing was that it never stopped. Soon I was back in San Francisco, gloating like crazy. I had made more than $50,000 in four weeks.

Then the fear set in. Everybody I knew was telling me I was nuts to hold on. It got to the point where the first word out of my brother's mouth every time I went to visit him at his software start-up was, "Sell!"

I was waking up in a cold sweat. What if I lost it all? If there's one thing more pathetic than reaching the end of a bull market and finding yourself still poor, it is reaching the end of a bull market and finding yourself ex-rich. Finally, for the sake of my health, I let it go at 140. It was the easiest money I'd ever made in my life. I was in the game. I was a player.

Four months later, eBay hit 700.

CHAPTER THREE

ABNORMAL PSYCHOLOGY

7:30 A.M. PST

One hour into the trading day the word spreads: E*Trade is down. In chat windows and message board discussions, the hard-core traders express their delight or dismay. We look at the E*Traders, along with their comrades-in-arms at discount Web-based brokerages like Discover Brokerage and Schwab.com and DLJ Direct, much in the same way the class bully used to regard that quiet, funny kid in fifth grade who had to be rescued by the playground monitor from the jungle gym. E*Traders are slow. E*Traders are credulous. E*Traders are pathetic. E*Traders are *E*Tards, and sometimes *l'users,* and sometimes, most derisively, *investors.*

And yet the E*Traders are necessary and welcome. Whenever I do something dumb—which is to say whenever I do something—they do something dumber. They are easy to take advantage of, because they are easy to understand. I just think back to what I used to do when I was an E*Trader.

After my experience with eBay, I became the well-pleased proprietor of a six-figure trading account. There were many demands on this money. I could pay off the debt on my car. I could get that laser surgery on my eyes in the United States rather than in Mexico City like I'd been planning. "Shoot," I said to myself, "this is *small-time* thinking." With my eBay profits, I could put a down payment on a shoebox of a condominium, just like my friends were doing. If I felt like I was ready to really turn over a new leaf, I could even pay back some of the money they'd loaned me.

It was fun having cash in my trading account. There were so many possibilities and options. I wiggled the fingers of my right hand on my chin, thinking hard. Hmmm . . . The world of E*Trade, unlike the bewildering environment of the true day trader, is not a hodgepodge of competing services and gadgets but a friendly, supportive nursery school for novices, where all your data needs are attended to, albeit loosely, and all your informational nourishment is presented in easy-to-digest chunklets. An E*Trade portfolio is set up to quickly summarize the movement of the most active stocks, and you can launch a tiny window containing a custom list, with gainers in green and losers in red. It was fun to check in every few minutes and see how my fortune was doing.

Since I was now so wealthy, I didn't feel especially obligated to pay close attention at my day job. In fact, it would be fair to say that I paid no attention at all. When my phone rang, I ignored it. E-mail queued up in my inbox until I thoughtfully created an auto-reply that read: "Sorry for the short answer—I'm tied up with something. Hope to be more free later this week or next, and I'll reply more intelligently." This struck exactly the right note—it didn't seem excessively generic, and might actually have been written on the fly. Given the thousands of e-mails that flew around our company—most containing information that was obsolete before it was sent—I gambled that this would take care of 99 percent of the people who thought they needed to communicate with me. The others could come try and find me in person. Anybody who dropped by my desk would see me staring dutifully at my computer, obviously deeply engaged in important tasks.

At this point in my trading career, I thought E*Trade was the cat's pajamas. Like an alcoholic who orders a double scotch and lets it sit on the bar in front of him for a long five minutes, enjoying the prospect of the bender to come, I skipped around on the E*Trade site for days, mentally jingling my $100,000.

One morning, I was alone in the office at six-thirty watching the first minutes of the market. E*Trade had a partnership with briefing.com, and every time you hit a button and refreshed the quotes on the stocks you were watching, you would also see the latest news on stocks in play that day. Most of the news was meaningless to me. Still, even a novice could see that briefing.com was a momentum booster. A stock earned mention when it began to move, and the mention would move it further. Then it would get mentioned again.

Suddenly, I had a *brilliant* idea. What would happen if I sat on my portfolio page at E*Trade, reloading every ten seconds, and bought some breakout stock the minute briefing.com posted it, and sold it after the run? No sooner said than done. I trained my attention on the headlines, waiting to ambush a gainer. I felt extremely clever, perched on the edge of my chair and using my index finger to poke at the left button of my mouse. Reload. Reload. Reload. Come on! Let's make some money!

The big moment came almost immediately. After three or four minutes of snapping my Nicorette and pressing away, *bang:*

10:05 ET Internet Movers: Infonautics (INFO 3 7/8 + 1 1/2, +63%), Greg Manning Auctions (GMAI 16 +5 17/32, +53%), Globix Corp (GBIX 10 +3 5/16, +50%), go2net (GNET 43 3/4 +14 1/4, +48%), EarthWeb (EWBX 78 5/8 +9 3/8, +14%), Netopia (NTPA 7 13/16 +2 3/16, + 39%), K-tel International Inc. (KTEL 24 1/8 −3 7/8, −14%).

These were some great stocks—some of them were up 50 percent or more in just the first few hours of trading. But how could I know which stock was the best one for the first live, without-a-net execution of my new, highly technical momentum-investment strategy?

When in doubt, go with strength. One minute later I picked the first one on the list—INFO—surfed to the trading screen, plugged in a market order for 3000 shares, and listened to the blood rush to my head. This was obviously a huge mistake. Before I could exhale, I vowed to reverse direction on this fool's path I was taking, and jumped over to my pending-orders page, plugging in a cancellation order. It was too late. A few reloads later, I had a confirmation icon flashing. Before my initial order could be erased, I'd bought 2400 shares.

The confirmation contained some not particularly joyous information. Infonautics wasn't selling for $3\frac{7}{8}$ anymore. My first 200 shares were bought at $6\frac{15}{32}$. My second 200 shares cost me $8\frac{5}{8}$. It went on like that until I got my last execution for 1000 shares at $8\frac{3}{4}$. I hadn't gotten on the bus first. I hadn't gotten on the bus second. I stuffed myself into this rattletrap at the last second before the doors closed, and I felt a suffocating attack of claustrophobia coming on. I had fled back to my trading page and put in an order to sell all 2400 shares. As I gripped my tongue between my teeth, trying to awaken myself from what I hoped was a dream, I punched at the reload button wildly.

At last, the alert icon lit up. When I clicked through, I found that I'd sold all 2400 shares. Between my purchase of this fine company and my sale of it, the stock had risen to $9\frac{1}{2}$. In less than two minutes, trading in a style indistinguishable from that of a second-grader with attention deficit disorder, I'd made $4,305. When I managed to slow my breath and check INFO's current price, it was below 8. My hands were trembling. My underpants were damp. I was ecstatic. This was easier than making money off of eBay. I didn't even know what Infonautics was.

An hour or so later, my superiority to other traders was confirmed by a briefing.com update:

> 11:59 ET Internet Stocks: Traders digging up some of the chart toppers from the April-May Internet frenzy. While these stocks are up big now, some traded at much higher levels earlier in the session. For example, the person(s) who purchased (and are still holding) Infonautics (INFO 6 13/16 + 4 7/16, +186%) at its $10.50 intraday high have seen the stock retreat 35% on them.

Not me, man. I was in early. I was playing the game like a pro. I started rich, and I ended richer.

At this point I started to have intimations that a whole different philosophy of life was available to me. I used to be one of those people who looked upon the world as a place that was chaotic, random, and not fair, where the spoils didn't go to the most deserving, and where complete nincompoops ended up getting paid. For the first time I understood that the wonderful thing about having a big pile of money drop into your lap for no reason was that you *didn't care in the slightest* if people thought you were a nincompoop.

Little did I know that, as an E*Trade customer with a six-figure account, I had a very specific function in the hierarchy of traders. My job was to buy the stocks they were selling, and sell the stocks they were buying. I was there to provide the liquidity. I was there to provide the money. Without me, and without those who replaced me, the retail intraday trading market—the world of the day traders—would have closed for business and turned out its lights a long, long time ago.

After all, a revolution is not a tea party.

You can't make an omelet without breaking some eggs.

Thank you, sir, may I have another?

Why have so few, in the history of our moralistic society, spoken out against the exploitation of idiots? Someday, a great gathering of the unintelligent will take place, and by their sheer numbers and the intensity of their resentment they—we—will sweep the institutions of finance away like so much dust on the glossy cover of an annual report.

Every so often, during my E*Trade days, I would receive an annual report in the mail. I never opened a single one. I preferred, during those months, to get my information from the great central plazas of the feebleminded, also known as the online message boards of Yahoo. After briefing.com, that's where I went for ideas.

It didn't used to be so easy to find a hundred thousand suckers. Before the Internet, you had to tout your low-float stocks via carefully nurtured lists of newsletter subscribers, or pay the rent on a fifth-floor walk-up full of ragged salesmen on telephones, cold-calling their way into a mile-deep hole of karmic debt. "If you don't want to make money," sneered the old-style telephone pitchman to a recalcitrant boob, "then there's not much I can do to help you. But if you *do* want to make money . . ."

I pretend to know better now, but I still find the online message boards fascinating. Just the other day, during a dull moment, I flitted over to the Yahoo discussion of PUBSF (also known as Elephant&Castle), a struggling Canadian restaurant operator whose stock had peaked at 11 sometime back in the Pleistocene era, on an announcement that they had signed a partnership with Disney to open a chain of Rainforest Cafes north of the border. This was followed by a short, sickening slide to about 5 dollars, and then by a longer sickening slide down to its recent level of about seventy-five cents, shedding waves of palsied shareholders along the way. The pain was terrible but apparently not fatal, for you will still find survivors on the Yahoo boards sharing inside information about upcoming earnings reports. They are greeted with dispirited, semi-consoling remarks to the effect of "It can't get any worse" and "One thing's for certain, it's up or out."

The finance boards on Yahoo are the most active community site anywhere on the Web and make up more than 60 percent of Yahoo's total traffic. Or so someone once told me. Rather than go to the trouble of looking up the statistics, I prefer to make this more or less logical but quite probably incorrect assertion and challenge you to prove me wrong. After all, that's how things are done on the Yahoo message boards.

No subject is more perfectly suited to all-day second-hand gossip than the stock market, with its cast of thousands of listed companies whose fortunes rise and fall in response to political, economic, and cultural news; the peccadilloes of executives; the announcement of partnerships made and broken; the weather. Jamie Tarses, the ex-president of ABC, once said that the secret to success on television is "to have a character who is very relatable, whom you root for." *Relatable* is a great word, and I'm sure she was speaking the truth, but the problem with ABC television is that it tries to do this with *people*. This is unnecessarily complicated. The audience on Yahoo has a stronger, more enduring bond—often masochistic—with the market's protagonists, and when they lose interest in one of the highly relatable characters, such as Netscape (NSCP), they instantly take up another, like Priceline (PCLN).

Even better, like on Jerry Springer, the audience is part of the show. Many of the most widely enjoyed personalities of the online finance discussion boards first met on the Prodigy online service, where a collection of active traders passed along tips about the movement of small-cap stocks. Many of the traders were savvy retail customers of discount brokerages who made decent money by spotting multiday trends. Many others traded penny stocks on the notorious Vancouver exchange.* It was difficult to get widespread publicity for penny stocks, which were rarely covered by the mainstream financial press, but the Prodigy boards offered a modern version of the classic pump-and-dump: the goal was to get a stock you owned to run up at least slightly on the enthusiasm you

---

* The Vancouver Stock Exchange was founded in 1907 and is managed for the benefit of the brokerage firms that own it and the promoters who encourage speculation in the stocks traded there. Many of these stocks carry prices of less than a dollar per share. The exchange has a reputation for profiting from the avarice of the ill-informed.

generated through your predictions of an imminent Pentecost, and then sell as the price rose. If all went well, you got rid of all your shares near the peak.

The atmosphere on Prodigy was contentious, especially when Tom and David Gardner showed up and began taunting the players. In those days, the Gardners were unknown promoters of an investment newsletter called *The Motley Fool,* and in the context of the Prodigy boards they seemed to have a bizarre style. For one thing, they were opposed to the active trading of stocks. The Gardners—who became known as the Fools—were interested in daily stock action as a spectator sport and as a source of ideas, but they had nothing but contempt for day traders. The Fools' satirical invention of a fake company called Zeigletics, a septic-accessories company with a growing business in Central Africa ("Chad is at the dawn of its Septic Age, and Zeigletics is the only player in the region") earned the Fools flattering mention in *The Wall Street Journal* and *Forbes,* along with quite a bit of counter-ridicule from the active traders on Prodigy, who didn't appreciate the caricature.

"The Prodigy days were really the Wild West," laughed Reverend Shark, a trader who helped chase the Gardner brothers off Prodigy. "The Fools were flamed right, left, and upside-down."

I tracked Reverend Shark down by telephone at his poolside office on Anna Maria Island, off the Florida coast, where he still earns his living trading stocks and selling advice to other traders. "It was not a friendly environment," he told me. "They got no respect there and they knew they never would." What really got under the Reverend's skin was that the Fools lumped all kinds of traders together, and didn't acknowledge the difference between the pump-and-dump penny-stock manipulators and the more serious technical traders like him. The Fools condemned all active traders who attempted to predict short-term movements of stock prices using the timeworn tools of momentum analysis. The fact that such tools might be difficult to use successfully did not mean they were useless. "The Fools really dumbed down the investment process," the Reverend complained.

But still, when the Gardner brothers and their Foolish followers decamped to America Online hoping to find a more sympathetic audience, the Reverend went along. Though he had chosen his name as an explicit rebuke to the Fools' anti-speculator sermons, he couldn't resist the gathering crowds on AOL. The Gardner brothers were moving online stock discussion into the mainstream— and becoming the first online celebrities in the process. This was a great boon to AOL, as the Motley Fool area became one of the company's most popular offerings.

With the rise of The Motley Fool, AOL's stock discussions began to show signs of a four-way split. The Gardners proclaimed a message of long-term hope. They even spoke up for the most boring investment strategy ever invented, the so-called Dogs of the Dow, popularized by money manager Michael O'Higgins in his book, *Beating the Dow.* Higgins argued that by using simple rules to select a few large-cap companies that were out of favor with investors, individuals could pound both the Dow index and most mutual fund managers while spending only about fifteen minutes per year analyzing their investments. For the people with a bit more time on their hands, the Gardners advocated a strict value approach; they seemed to believe that investors should actually know what a company did, be familiar with its financial statements, and have an opinion about the prospects for growth in its industry.

Against the Gardners stood the technical traders and position traders like Reverend Shark. The Reverend had been a tax attorney and certified public accountant in the late eighties, but when he began to lose his hearing he closed his law practice and started trading stocks full-time. His favorite strategy was to keep an eye on low-cap companies that had some good news to announce, good news that he would find by doing online research and reading analysts' reports. He would build a position, and when the stock jumped he'd get out. This was simple, enjoyable, and lucrative.

Alongside the value investors—the Fools—and the active traders—the Sharks—there was a third group: the delirious touts. Many of these were not even the professional touts of the old Prodigy days but simply energetic pump-and-dump amateurs who would build a position in a small stock and blow the horn until they could escape with some free money. The loudest or most creative touts would gather a little following, a loosely organized pump-and-dump alliance. For instance, the much loved Waco Kid, using a subtle reverse-psychology strategy, would announce a stock pick and proclaim that this information was "embargoed" and not to be disclosed to anybody outside the "Waco Kid organization." Meanwhile TokyoJoe, aka TokyoMex, aka Paku Matsudai, aka Yun Soo Oh Park, was sending machine-gun blasts of misspelled enthusiasm about his favorite high flyers.

One day I tracked down TokyoJoe through his Web site and gave him a call. I suspected he would not object to a direct question. "Why hype stocks?" I asked.

"The stock market is all hype," he answered, "whether you are a day trader or Merrill Lynch. One hypes on the Internet, one in a Brooks Brothers suit." The rumors that TokyoJoe was selling shares into the buying runs prompted by his relentless posting didn't hurt his ability to gain a following—quite the contrary. You didn't have to believe anything he wrote in order to take it as a signal, as long as you assumed other, slower readers would take it as a buying signal, too. And since so many people wanted in on the game—as long as they were in early—a subgenre of the pump-and-dump post was the pump-and-dump post aimed at other pump-and-dump posters. This style of posting still occurs today. For instance:

> To: TokyoMex who wrote (78030)
> From: Goldbug Guru Sunday, Jun 6 1999 9:35PM ET
> Respond to Post # 78040 of 96440
>
> TokyoMex & all!
> The latest Hot Stocks on Wall Street is HIGH SPEED
> ACCESS (HSAC). Check it out my friend, this stock will

move big time in the next couple of months. You guys are looking at a 100% to 800% return on your investment. Both Daytraders & Investors will love to get their hands on HSAC on Monday. Go with the flow! HSAC will be the hottest trading stock on nasdaq in the coming days, get in early before the low price is all gone.

BUY HSAC!

Who knows? Maybe somebody did buy HSAC. Goldbug Guru made his post on Sunday. HSAC had gone public on the previous Wednesday, and on Friday, before the hype began, it had closed at about 20. The following Monday it climbed to 24 and then began to sink, dropping to 16 in a week. If Goldbug Guru got out on the morning after he made this post, he did well. The credulous were punished.

The fourth class of online stock discussion participants consisted of the majority of bewildered readers and occasional posters whose motivations for participating were opaque. Why were they here? For entertainment? For information? For advice? If they wanted entertainment, they were perfectly placed; if they wanted information, they were victims-in-waiting; if they believed the advice, they were crazy. And yet, at the beginning of the great bull market, people of all different trading styles were making money, and Reverend Shark thought the Gardners were being plain ridiculous to deny that day trading was successful for at least some of the better practitioners.

"Why don't you be honest and say that there are other

methodologies?" Reverend Shark asked the Fools, whom he never tired of provoking. "You may not use them, but they work for other people."

When I asked him the same question, David Gardner explained that there were two reasons he and his brother were so antagonistic to the active traders. "One is that we don't believe they perform very well," he said. "You are paying capital gains taxes every time you cash out, and there's the commissions and other friction costs as well." But the other reason was less financial than philosophical. "Also, you have no life. I mean, you know, get out there and go to the beach! Get away from the market. Go talk to people. I think there are going to be people who twenty years from now look back and say, 'You know, I wish I hadn't spent my time sitting in front of my computer clicking the left mouse button.' So when you combine the notion that you are spending your whole life to do worse than you would have done if you had just bought and held . . . . " Gardner laughed. "Well, obviously, there are just a whole bunch of jokes that could be made based on concepts like that."

"Hardy har har, who's laughing now," I say to myself, mentally spending the additional cash I intend to make in the next few hours. For every dollar I make in the market, I spend ten in my imagination. This is a bad habit I have never been able to shake.

The morning has been a little inactive, I admit; though the market is jumping up I keep seeing the bargains disappear in front of my face. Money is shifting back into hardware, says a gray-suited gentleman on CNBC. This makes me laugh again. We've come full circle. Back at the dawn of the day-trading age, not only were online traders of every style making money but they were all making money in the same high tech hardware stock: Iomega.

In 1995, the price for a share of this small Utah disk drive company ran up from 3½ to more than 50. The people on the Motley Fool message boards were playing it all the way. I asked David Gardner if there wasn't a contradiction, or at least a bit of irony, in the fact that the origin of The Motley Fool will forever be associated with the bull run on Iomega. His answer was no. "We bought at a split-adjusted price of two dollars and never sold it. The problem with Iomega was that they couldn't execute, but they created a product that people really wanted and that was deployed across millions of computers. They are not akin to the crappy, rinky-dink companies that are pure speculation."

The Gardner brothers made some money on Iomega, even at today's price of 3½. Reverend Shark made a lot of money off this stock, trading it all the way up. TokyoJoe doesn't like to talk about the stock. "Iomega sucks!" he complained to Cory Johnson, a reporter at The Street.com who interviewed him a few years ago. And somewhere out there are thousands of Americans who bought Iomega at its peak and got killed. Many of them were enthusiastic followers of The Motley Fool.

There was no doubt that playing this game could get

you hurt. Iomega was situated at the scary point where multiple social and technological waves combined. In 1994 the personal computer business, which had paused briefly to catch its breath, was accelerating again with the advent of the Internet. Faster chips led to more complicated programs and bigger files, which Iomega's digital storage products could handle. The Gardners were right: the company looked like a winner.

But it wasn't just Iomega's products that were well positioned, it was also their stock. With the '87 crash receding in the rearview mirror, the financial press was searching for an explanation for the healthy market of the mid-nineties. They found one that any dope could understand: the postwar generation was funneling billions into retirement accounts, which meant mutual funds, which meant demand for securities, which meant stock prices were rising. Meanwhile, the philosophy of Peter Lynch— buy what you know—influenced celebrated investment clubs, such as the Beardstown Ladies, which in turn encouraged millions of retail investors to use their own habits and observations as a guide to what stocks to buy. And finally, by 1994, the online services were providing a feedback mechanism through which amateurs could share research and thus influence each other. This is what happened in the AOL discussion of Iomega. One of the regular participants drove by the company's headquarters in Utah and noticed that the parking lot was full. This led to a little research, which led to eager discussion, which led to buying, which led to press coverage, which led to more online discussion, which led to more buying. *Feedback*. Like the sound of a microphone placed near a loudspeaker, the manic squeal grew louder and louder. During eighteen months of wild speculation, which peaked in May 1996, Iomega rose by more than 7,000 percent.

Subsequent Internet-enabled bull runs on high tech stocks have dwarfed even the enthusiasm for Iomega in its heyday, but the run on Iomega has become the classic cautionary tale of the Internet trading culture. The name of the company is repeated like a mantra whenever a newly discovered high tech favorite begins to catch the interest of retail buyers. When I'd spoken with David Gardner, I hadn't been able to resist challenging him a little more about The Motley Fool's contribution to the Iomega debacle: Despite all of the Gardners' very reasonable instruction, didn't The Motley Fool function as the first great, online stock market racing sheet? Didn't the Fools help everybody learn to think about the stock market as a kind of sporting event?

Gardner didn't mind the metaphor, but he objected to the implicit criticism. He expressed surprise that the American public had ever allowed itself to be diverted by sports, when stock investing was competitive, exciting, *and* lucrative. "If we're being charged with making the market entertaining, I think that's a good thing. You could put that on my gravestone," he said.

By 1998, when I arrived on the scene, the divergent evolutionary branches of the stock discussion boards flourished in several distinct environments—though there was plenty of overlap and competition for resources. The value investors were most comfortable at The Motley Fool. The technical and position traders favored Silicon Investor. And the aimless hordes liked Yahoo, which was free, completely anonymous, and minimally managed. As for the touts, they were everywhere.

I always read all the sites, trying the get the drift of the boobs. This is as much an art as a science, like so many of the skills of a great speculator. I remember my first killing from the Yahoo boards, which I owe to a great river of boobosity known as sector analysis. Sector analysis involves identifying the root causes of the movement of a lead stock, and then playing other stocks in the same business. This seems obvious, but because of the way companies are organized, it is often unclear where to find the secondary gainers after the lead company has gone up big time. This is particularly true in the always attractively volatile Internet sector, where today's car dealership is tomorrow's online bank.

After eBay went to the moon, there was quite a bit of interest in finding other e-commerce companies that might be likely to issue a press release in the near future announcing that they were considering competing with eBay someday. After a few days of lucubration, my message board friends at Yahoo discovered Creative Computers, whose symbol was MALL. Incredibly, the company had recently filed to spin off its online subsidiary, uBid, a site that auctioned surplus and refurbished computer goods.

Hey! Did someone say *auction*?! Never mind the fact

that neither the parent company nor its stepchild had much by way of users or profits. Creative Computers owned an online auction site. And not only that. That auction site was going to be spun off and taken public. And not only that, people close to people in the company had been sharing definite if not entirely concrete suggestions that some portion of uBid shares would be distributed to the shareholders of MALL.

This looked like a once-in-a-lifetime opportunity. The rumors hit, conveniently enough, on the same day that theglobe.com, an online community site, went public, setting a record for the biggest first-day gain in Nasdaq history. This gain was almost entirely due to theglobe.com's having been the first Internet IPO after eBay.

Anyone who bought theglobe.com at its early peak of 97 and saw it crater to 63½ by the end of the day had learned the hard way that this wasn't how to get in on a hot Internet IPO. You had to somehow be an insider and acquire the shares at the offering price, or less. Maybe buying MALL would be an easy way to become an insider and beat the first-day rush. MALL started moving.

Between the Yahoo boards and briefing.com, I was one in-the-know day trader. I waited to be certain the trend was real, and I bought MALL after its second briefing.com mention: 1000 shares at 24. The next thing I knew it was up to 28. Another instant killing.

Why didn't I sell immediately? Maybe I really thought I'd wait for those uBid shares. Maybe I wanted to push my luck a little. Or maybe I just felt comfortable chewing the fat with my online brethren. To be honest, I can't really explain why I remained an owner of MALL. In any case, I decided to let my profits run.

Now that I had $28,000 in the game I was constantly in search of reassurance, and I spent several long sessions every day reading the MALL thread. The discussion was positively medieval. Math was calculated painstakingly and repeatedly. I learned of a purported distribution formula, something like .6656 UBID shares for every MALL share held. Everybody got busy making premature imaginary valuation calculations. How much should MALL be worth if we assume it has an inherent value of 15 and UBID, once spun off, trades at 80? What if MALL's inherent worth is only 10? Sure, but what if UBID trades at 100? or 200?

One question that was never asked: What if neither MALL nor UBID has any value whatsoever? This wasn't the time for querulous criticism. This was the hour of glory. This was the birth of a new concept in the stock market: the IPO tracking stock. The IPO tracking stock is the stock of a company which is about to spin off another company with an (at least hypothetical) Internet business. The IPO-tracking-stock manipulation would later be repeated to great effect when Navarre spun off its NetRadio unit, when Barnes & Noble spun off barnesandnoble.com, and when Ziff-Davis spun off ZDNet. The ZDNet scheme produced the bizarre spectacle of a nearly wholly owned spin-off valued by the public market at a figure higher than the value of the company that owned most of it.

This was the stock market as painted by M. C. Escher, and I absolutely could not resist. A week later I bought 1000 more shares of MALL at 34. The next day, in a bizarre attack of rationality, I sold at 38½ and took my profits, which amounted to more than $18,000.

I sold too soon. It kept rising. By the time I got back in for 1000 shares later that day, the price was 47. It broke through 50. And then the market closed. It was Thanksgiving, a four-day weekend. In the middle was a half-day of trading on Friday, wherein MALL blew through 60 and then began to drop. When the half-day finished, it was in the mid-50s and I was worried. Over the weekend I watched the discussion. There were fewer cheerleaders now, and the ones who remained wore their ignorance on their sleeves. Suddenly, people seemed to remember that the companies in play were jokes and always had been. Even I could tell that the party was over.

I visualized MALL back at 24 before the end of the next weekday. With turkey leftovers smeared across my face and a wishbone tucked into my CD-ROM drive, I knelt before my machine and prayed that I'd be given a chance to get out of MALL first thing Monday before the bottom dropped out.

My prayers were answered. When I woke up the next day, the stock was making another run. As the stock rose halfheartedly, I put in a sell order at 57. Minutes later, madly clicking E*Trade's refresh button, I saw it sail downward through 57. Hmmm. Had I sold? There was no confirmation from E*Trade. Now it was really moving. There was nobody left to buy this flying pig. Where was my confirmation? It kept going down to 54, 52, 49, 45. Half an hour later it was in the low 40s and I still didn't have my confirmation. Was I in or out? Every point below 47 cost me $1,000. Didn't they understand? I had to know whether my trade had been executed. But there was no way to get through. CNBC was reporting: E*Trade site down again. When I tried to call, the line was busy. I was going to give back every dime I'd made on this stock. Desperate traders told stories of driving all the way down to the E*Trade offices in the Valley and begging for confirmation. Of recruiting dozens of friends to join with them in collective redialing. Of attempting to communicate through smoke signals.

A little bit of my mind was lost that day. While desperately trying to get E*Trade on the line, I felt my eyes watering and a strange, puffy feeling developing in my sinuses. When I dabbed at my face with a Kleenex, I pulled it away to find it soaked with blood. There was a red rivulet gushing from my nose and tears of frustration streaming from my eyes. My girlfriend was crouched in the corner, her hand over her mouth, trying to figure out whether to call 911 or a priest. She reached for the phone. "Don't touch that!" I screamed.

At that moment, my confirmation alert showed up. I was out at 57. MALL was currently trading at 42. Not only had I made another $10,000 but *everybody else had lost.* Holding hands and nuzzling one another like kittens, my girlfriend and I lunched in South Park that day. I swear to God there was a rainbow.

I couldn't handle something like that happening again.

I was convinced I had become a genius trader, but my tools weren't holding up to my pace. The next day, I tried to transfer all my money out of my E*Trade account. The transfer-funds function was busted. After three consecutive days on hold, I got someone from E*Trade on the line and gave him my bank's routing number. How much did I want to transfer out? All of it, please. I was leaving the boobs behind.

CHAPTER FOUR

A HIGHER LEVEL

8:30 A.M. PST

Y ou can't really do what I'm doing now—evaluating stocks every minute—using E*Trade. But what I've gained in speed, I've lost in simplicity.

The ordinary Web-based discount stock site, such as E*Trade, is about as complicated as a Tickle Me Elmo. You have nothing to fear, other than the indescribable psychic agony of wondering what could possibly have happened to an order that represents most of your net worth, or more. The same user-friendliness cannot be ascribed to E*Trade's sadistic older cousin, the much licensed trading application known as Real Tick III.

Real Tick III, created by Townsend Analytics, offers home traders access to detailed information about buy and sell orders. While amateur traders surf their accounts on E*Trade and Schwab, punching in orders on sluggish

Web pages, day traders everywhere—from bedroom desk-tops to metropolitan trading shops—plug directly into the market with Real Tick III, which is programmed to breath-lessly suck the ever shifting universe of data we know as the stock market onto one's machine, and spit the not-so-occasional order back out into the market. There's no Web surfing or hitting the reload button with Real Tick III; Real Tick III *is* the reload button.

Traders who use Real Tick III speak of having access to "Level II." In Nasdaq parlance, Level I refers to the most basic information: the highest bid and the lowest ask for a stock. Level II shows you every bid and ask, along with its source.

I have never ceased to marvel at Real Tick III. Of the many near-miraculous uses for modern digital technol-ogy, the most dazzling is its capacity for simulation. Sev-eral years ago, I went down to Redwood City to visit Jaron Lanier, the inventor of virtual reality, and when he strapped his experimental goggles on my head and pushed me up into the simulated clouds, I felt a wave of genuine wonder. Level II evokes a similar feeling. Though at first view Level II is merely a confusing jumble of num-bers, with the soundtrack provided by CNBC you can achieve the illusion of complete immersion in one of the most awful environments on the planet: a stock market trading floor.

Unlike the small cadre of day traders who rent comput-ers, software, and an Internet connection from a day-trading office, I trade alone at home. I want my privacy.

Maybe some people enjoy sitting on a wobbly chair in a musty room full of traders, but the last thing I need is the three-hundred-pound hotshot at the terminal next to me convulsing in ripples of giggles as I sputter curses at my disobedient momentum plays. Or for the floor manager to be calling me into his office, urging me to stick to the All-Trade E-Z Pro Stochasto Method if I really want to survive. Or worst of all, having my home-run days ruined by the sound of choked sobbing underneath the desk behind me, where another ruined trader is finding solace from the market and her peers. No, no, no fucking way. Trading always involves the risk of losing; and losing, at least in this era, in this country, always has something furtive and shameful about it. Eventually you wrap up the shame in a "funny" story. But at the moment the whip comes down, I want my door to be closed.

Another benefit of remote trading, of course, is the ability to choose your own software and trading rig, unconstrained by the whims of some budget-minded office manager. Before deciding on Real Tick III, I browsed the features lists and played with demos of the competitors, such as The Watcher and Cybertrader. These Level II software packages all seemed fundamentally similar. Even though many of the trading shops use their own software, most of the alpha traders on the discussion boards endorsed Real Tick III, and who was I to argue?

Today I have six Level II windows set across three extra-large monitors, each window dedicated to its own Nasdaq stock. The windows are about four inches square, and below each I've placed a real-time chart showing stock prices at one-minute intervals. This produces a bizarre psychological illusion. Every time a stock ticks up, I have an almost physical conviction that I know in advance what is going to happen. Right now, waiting for the next tick, I can feel the correct answer just at the edge of my consciousness. I know it, but I can't quite articulate it.

Ah, I've got it—but now it's too late, because the number has already appeared on my screen.

The numbers continue to flash by—rising and hesitating and then rising again and hesitating and then falling, no, rising again—and it occurs to me that digital simulations are used to introduce students or trainees to something that they are not yet ready to handle in reality. The weeklong, round-the-clock, all-hands-on-deck battle simulations the U.S. military stages for its reserves are a great way to get people accustomed to having their fingers on the trigger, and to pulling the trigger, without anyone actually getting killed. Perhaps it would be best for all concerned if these military exercises never got beyond the simulation stage, and the same could be said of Level II trading. With a few well-publicized exceptions, it doesn't leave traders dead, but Level II's capacity to help you get scalped, taken out, whipsawed, and hacked to pieces is breathtaking.

My Real Tick III screen has all the tools I could dream of, and more: constantly updated quotes, streaming charts, refreshed news headlines, real-time sorting. No need to click on the reload button every thirty seconds to see if my stock has appeared on briefing.com—the basic lemming play is automatically dropped into my lap by Real Tick. Even so, it's not the data flow that justifies the base rate of $250 per month I pay to Townsend Analytics. What I'm really after are instant executions. Instant as in less than five seconds, less than two seconds, he clicks he scores, right now, *instant.*

The promise of instant execution is what has made day trading plausible. If you're going to be in and out of a stock in less than a minute, every second counts. Gone are the days when you phoned your order into a broker and he sent it to a specialist on the floor of the New York Stock Exchange and the specialist wrote it down in his book and made the trade when he damn well pleased. When I type my order into the computer, I want it done. Now.

There's a catch to instant executions, though: you have to make choices for yourself. This reduces the number of people you can blame when the trade becomes hopelessly messed up. I'm looking at my Real Tick windows at this moment. For each stock, there are columns showing the current price; the bids to buy stocks and the offers to sell them; the day's volume; the high and low price for the day; and yesterday's closing price. An arrow shows whether the stock has ticked up or down. All the current bids sit in the left column, the best on top, the worst at the bottom. They are color coded, with all bids at the same price sharing one color: yellow, green, light blue, red, dark blue, cycling back to yellow, and so on. The asks sit on the right, with the cheapest on top and the most expensive at the bottom. Next to each bid and ask there's a four-letter code showing the brokerages and trading networks that are posting orders.

I'm often watching Lycos, since I'm an inadvertent investor in the company, which became the owner of my Web site, Suck, when Wired Ventures, the old owner, was split up and sold. Showing bids and offers for Lycos are GSCO (Goldman Sachs), MSCO (Morgan Stanley), and MLCO (Merrill Lynch). There are also bids coming through several electronic communications networks, or ECNs. Instinet (INCA) is the oldest ECN and is used by big institutional traders. Island (ISLD) and Archipelago (ARCA) are the ones most popular with day traders. An order of less than 1000 shares that comes through Island or Archipelago is almost certainly a day trader's order. This is important for me to know, because when it is mostly other traders playing a stock, you can count on some movement up or down. Day traders have their hand on the trigger all the time.

Learning which ECNs to use and how to read them is preposterously complicated. Everybody has their favorite method of entry and exit. The problem, and it is hardly a trivial problem, is that moving against the momentum is a lot easier than moving with it. If you're buying when everyone is selling or selling when everyone is buying, no problem. But who wants to do that? Not me. I'm not a long-term investor. My goal is to beat the crowd by a few seconds, both going in and getting out, and if I miss my chance because of a bad execution, well, here's what happens.*

Not long ago the stock price of an Internet search company I follow—call it InfoSphinx (SPHX)—had been lolling around for weeks at about 50. Then Ask Jeeves, another search site, announced earnings that weren't quite as bad as analysts expected. On this dose of good news, which was really a dose of slightly less bad news, Ask Jeeves shot up a few points in heavy trading. All the dumb money quickly found its way off the table in Jeeves, but the other search sites, I thought, would soon follow. So I watched, and waited, and then, by coincidence, Info-Sphinx dropped a press release on the wire announcing that they'd been chosen for a premium placement on the home page of chocolove.com, the e-commerce site for premium-chocolate lovers. This was a beautiful piece of nonnews and promised to have a predictable effect. I decided to grab 1000 shares of SPHX. The best offer I could see in my Real Tick window was at 49⅞, from Morgan Stanley. I'll take it, I thought.

No I won't—because just as I hit return, the Morgan Stanley quote disappeared. Somebody else had had the same thought. Then, for the briefest moment, there was another 49⅞ offer on Island, but that was gone before I was convinced it was even real. Instantly, there appeared a long column of 50s, straight down the screen. Plenty of

---

* Desperate intraday trading maneuvers can get complicated. This example is a simplified composite of a number of humiliating incidents.

offers, I thought, and went to hit one, but integers like 50 are very dangerous, because they are irresistible as limit orders and "stops," customer requests to trade a stock when it hits a specified price. There must have been tons of orders for SPHX at 50. As soon as they lined up on the right, they disappeared again.

And so I found myself engaged in the damaging activity known as chasing. Again and again I attempted to buy the stock, trying to remember, as my fingers flew, the rules governing the different ECNs. Island is the fastest, but you can't bid above the highest offers, and the highest offers were disappearing before I could hit them. I'd never catch up with the stock this way. On Archipelago, however, you can bid as high as you want for a stock. *Perhaps I should outrun the market a bit and let it catch up to me. I won't get the best price but at least I'll be in on the run.* Now the best offer was at 50⅞, and I'd lost a whole point, and before I even had time to swear, we hit 51 and a bunch of orders pushed it over the top to 51⅛. "Screw this," I said, finally getting my feeble curse out in a raspy whisper, and as 51⅛ disappeared I upped the ante by $250 and bid 51⅜ for 1000 shares on ARCA. Naturally, I got them just as the momentum slowed and the people who snaked me at 49⅞ figured that chocolove was not really one of the big players on the Internet scene, at least not yet, and that maybe a buck and a half was all they were going to get that morning. And if they went for 1000 shares, this gave them a quick profit of $1,500. So they jumped out, and the price started to fall, and now I was chasing it down. I offered to sell at 51⅛, at 51, at 50¾. This hurt, but it apparently didn't hurt enough, because some dumbasses playing this stock were bailing out so recklessly that the stock actually dropped *below* 49⅞, the original price, before my sell order was executed. Thus was I witness, once again, to the amazing and magical motion of stock actually dropping on unexpected good news. I had now been well and truly burned in both directions. Who was I going to blame? Easy. I blamed the computers. How did we get to the point where machines are allowed to trade stocks?

In May 1971, *Harper's* editor Louis Lapham had a conversation with Don Regan, the Merrill Lynch chairman who would one day run the Treasury Department for Ronald Reagan. Regan told Lapham that the New York Stock Exchange was doomed. "It's an anachronism," he said. "It hasn't emerged from the technology of the nineteenth century." The exchange would be replaced by a computer network, Regan predicted.

In late 1995, almost a quarter of a century after Regan spoke with Lapham about the end of Wall Street, a California technology company commissioned an ad to run in the U.S. edition of *The Wall Street Journal*. The headline read: "Your Broker Is Now Obsolete." The advertiser was E*Trade, which was about to launch Web-based trading for retail investors. E*Trade's Web site was developed by Pam Kramer, who had experience producing computer software aimed at children, and the company was extremely proud of its simple, two-click interface. Click,

click, and 100 shares of Microsoft Corporation were yours at 99 dollars a share.

Finally, you could give up worrying about whether your investment adviser was churning your account, because you could churn your account for yourself. What would this mean for vulnerable investors? Would easy access to buying and selling increase volatility, cause small-timers to go mad chasing profits, and ruin the innocent? In 1995, when the Dow had only recently shot above 6,000, there was rumored to be a new class of after-work traders who fooled themselves into thinking that the market would never stop rising. "Some investors have allowed visions of a 10,000 Dow to get in the way of common sense," observed a team of reporters in *USA Today,* shortly before E*Trade's site went live.

The Dow at 10,000? Oh, naïve prognosticators! You lacked imagination. For some reason the feeling I get looking back on 1995—that miracle year that brought so many obscure and illogical moneymaking strategies to light, many of them effective—is a feeling of terror. We didn't know. We honestly didn't know. The first Internet billionaires had yet to be minted. We still thought a million dollars was a lot of dough.

In 1995 I had my own plan for getting rich, and it wasn't through trading stocks. Only one year earlier I had been a semiskilled peon in the technology industry, helping soon-to-be bankrupt gaming companies produce computer-powered shoot-'em-ups. Then my luck had turned: I was the first one into the not-yet-peed-in pool of a sexy new profession: HTML jockey. In 1994, I had started liberating fools from their money in return for setting up their corporate Web sites, and by 1995 I'd wrangled my way into what I thought was a dream gig at *Wired* magazine's site, HotWired. My task was to take old stories from *Wired* and convert them into the proper format for display on the World Wide Web, under the supervision of a troubled genius named Carl Steadman. Carl had experience—he had already set up an online publishing system for his favorite magazine, *Critical Theory*, and he had also written a children's book about cats. Our boss, Andrew Anker, explained to us privately that when HotWired went public, we were all going to have so much money that everything that we had experienced earlier in our lives was going to seem like a pathetic joke. "Do you think you can handle this?" Andrew asked.

Maybe we couldn't. Because as the sparkling clear waters of our lightly chlorinated backyard pool party became more and more crowded with kids from the neighborhood, and from every neighborhood, we began to panic. Nineteen ninety-five was the year that everybody realized they needed a Web site. It was the year that Netscape went public, educating everybody in the industry about what this boom might mean. Launched at 27, Netscape shares hit 71 on the first day. Nineteen ninety-five was the year that saw the first Web-based travel site, the first Web-based soap opera, the first Web-based striptease emporium.

The change came too fast. We weren't prepared to com-

pete successfully with all the insanely eager business development executives who started coming around with a
pack of business plans they were able to summarize in
thirty seconds. They must have practiced by juggling marbles with their mouths, because at the first indication of
skepticism they could switch pitches mid-sentence and
sometimes even mid-word. Bored with rectifying the mar-
gins on the Wired Web site but too paralyzed by amazement to participate wholeheartedly in the gold rush, we
watched our fellow HTML jockeys spin the feeblest
threads of ideas into start-up gold. There was no end to
the development money showering down upon anybody
who could convincingly claim expertise, and the skunk-
works and greenhouse financiers were running around
like rabbits on Viagra, shooting a bounteous stream of
funding all over the best talkers.

If only we could have relaxed and enjoyed it. Today, we
probably would. But the atmosphere at Wired was serious—righteous even—and we looked upon the new Web
sites as ridiculous interlopers who were half-mad with
self-regard and doomed to fail. In fact, even while we
vaguely hoped that Wired would eventually make us rich,
we looked upon Wired itself as a ridiculous interloper,
half-mad and doomed to fail.

So, in a series of late-night marathons, Carl and I created Suck. Suck was our way to strike a blow against the
Web's crack-addled entrepreneurs. Maybe we suspected
that they'd all succeed—the Netscapes and Real Audios
and Cnets and Pathfinders and HotWireds—and if that

was their fate, we wanted to humiliate them while we still had the chance. As we tried to build traffic, we made a delightful discovery: nobody liked to read cruel things about a company's misguided plans more than the very people charged with implementing those plans, i.e., the target company's employees. To guarantee our fame, we attacked the biggest domains. Nobody knew who we were, but for a very brief time, everybody knew the URL. The sorriest legacy of *that* was the slew of s-sites that followed in our wake. Before the letter *e* won lasting favor, new Web companies seemed to have a preference for the letter *s,* and we watched people burn piles of thousand-dollar bills on sites like Spiv, Stim, and The Spot.

Disintermediation—a neologism for "cutting out the middleman"—was company dogma at Wired, so Carl and I didn't feel any twinges of guilt about using HotWired's server to publish anonymous communications directly to its readers, outside the control of our editors and bosses. After all, everybody from the founder of the company down to the editorial assistants down to the tech support staff down to me was supposed to be liberating the world's media consumers from the narrow prejudices of the mainstream press. With Suck, Carl and I were only too happy to prove the point: by the mid-nineties any immature, reckless idiot could operate in a field previously open only to professionals. On the Internet, gatekeepers were obsolete. There was nobody to save us from ourselves.

Meanwhile, the mania for loony Internet schemes had been quietly crossbreeding with the stock market mania of the post-'87 bull run. Like a party that degenerates into a riot, the change happened in several distinct places simultaneously before spreading to engulf everybody. The profoundest effect of disintermediation would be seen not in the whorish world of advertising-supported media, where Carl and I were eagerly working, but in the holy capital of capitalism: Wall Street. Can you see me banging the heel of my hand against my head? *If I'd only known.*

When did the destruction of Wall Street become inevitable? Don Regan could see it in 1971. Instinet, the first system to allow buyers and sellers to trade directly, using computers, was created in 1969.* But perhaps the seeds of destruction were sown at the very beginning, when Manhattan traders gathered themselves into a circle under a tree and agreed to try to monopolize the market. Outsiders have been gunning for them ever since, and the Exchange seems to have met each modest suggestion of reform with a clear, crisp, kindergartenesque shake of the head and a loud exclamation of "Mine!"

Perhaps the most important day in the history of attacks on Wall Street insiders was May 1, 1975, the date Congress mandated the elimination of fixed commissions for trading stocks and the introduction of price competi-

---

* Instinet was the first ECN devoted to stock trading. It was created in the era of fixed commissions, when the biggest buyers and sellers of stocks—mutual funds, pension funds, and other institutions—were forced to pay huge prices to brokers when they made large trades. Because it allowed the institutions to trade directly with each other, Instinet was a money saver. While it allows institutions to bypass brokers, it was not designed for the retail market.

tion among brokers. The stock brokers of the Exchange, articulate advocates of capitalism in every other context, defended their monopoly up to the last moment. They called—and still call—the end of fixed commissions Mayday.

In *Revolution on Wall Street,* Marshall Blume, Jeremy Siegel, and Dan Rottenberg tell the story of the end of old-style price fixing on the Exchange, and they have preserved a delightful quote from a broker who appeared before the SEC to warn of dire consequences during the months leading up to Mayday. "Mayday is a great holiday in Russia," said the broker, soberly, "and Russia has said there is no need to fight democracy. It will burn itself out. Well, Commissioners, you have the candle and the matches, and it will be a short fuse." Miraculously, not only capitalism but also the New York Stock Exchange survived, and an explosion of stock trading even increased profits for brokerages who managed the transition.

Although the government succeeded in forcing the New York Stock Exchange to accept price competition for trades, it failed to pressure the exchange into creating a single, national, electronic system for price quotes and trading orders. Don Regan and others knew that networks of computers could theoretically match buyers and sellers without the intervention of brokers on the floor of the exchange, but there were several problems to overcome. One was the primitive state of computer technology. A national electronic stock market would have meant rooms

full of mainframes chugging away and talking to brokerages via buggy extranets. Now, at the dawn of a new
millennium, we can be grateful that the nation's entire
financial market isn't dependent on three decades of
hacked code written in COBOL.

Nonetheless, at the time, a national system appeared to
be feasible. In 1971 the National Association of Securities
Dealers created an automatic quote system for over-the-
counter stocks—stocks not listed on any exchange. Nasdaq, as the system was called, ran on two Univacs, and by
the end of the decade it was unquestionably the most important stock market for smaller companies seeking fi-
nancing from the public. Premonitions of an eventual
Y2K freak-out were not what stalled the invention of a national electronic market; rather, it was the dependable resistance of the members of the still-powerful Exchange,
which wanted to preserve some vestige of their monopoly
over the trading of listed stocks. After all, if stocks in
America's most successful public companies were bought
and sold via computer, what role would the broker on the
floor play? In place of a national market, the Exchange offered something called the Intermarket Trading System,
which allowed dealers to transfer buy and sell orders from
one market to another. Access to the Intermarket Trading
System was—and is still today—controlled by a commit-
tee of representatives of the established exchanges.

While Nasdaq flourished, the retail stock buyer was living in more or less the same world he or she had been living in since discount brokers like Charles Schwab came to
prominence after Mayday. But a new stage of disinterme-

diation was looming. At about the same time online companies like America Online began to market themselves to the mainstream, Bill Porter founded E*Trade securities. Porter had been running a deep-discount brokerage service bureau called Trade Plus, and in 1991 he used his profits from Trade Plus to create an online brokerage offering discount trades via dial-up modem, Touch-Tone phone, CompuServe, and AOL. Porter's trading system was automated, which meant his costs were radically lower than that of other brokerages. So were his fees. At a time when Charles Schwab was still charging $55 to trade 1000 shares, and fifty-five cents for each additional share, E*Trade was billing $19.95 for a trade of any size.

The company was instantly profitable. While brokers, programmers, and customer service staff couldn't be completely eliminated, the costs of maintaining the system grew much more slowly than the capacity to execute orders. Like eBay, which would arrive three years later, Porter had figured out how to automate the manufacture of money: A form appears on the screen; the customer fills it out; data is sent into the market; the trade is made; commission is deducted; confirmation is returned. Once the system was designed and programmed, trading volume could increase rapidly. E*Trade *scaled.*

As the signs of Internet fever began to emerge in 1995, E*Trade's volume exploded. Revenues went from less than $1 million in 1992 to more than $25 million in 1996. Toward the end of that year, the brokerage celebrated its millionth trade, and the service suffered its first devastating breakdown, as traders had to wait more than two hours during a system crash. After the crash, E*Trade paid $1.7 million in make-good money. But still the site flourished. Better yet, E*Trade went public. In August E*Trade stock was issued at 10½ per share, and seven months later it had risen by 150 percent—and the biggest leaps, by far, were still to come. Christopher Byron, a financial columnist for *The New York Observer* who loved to pour cold water on new Internet issues, made an exception for E*Trade. "Open up an E*Trade account," he wrote, "and make your first purchase a block of the company's shares."

I was all too familiar with the work of Chris Byron. Wired was also scheduled to go public in the fall of 1996. In respect to the company in which I owned a tiny but, to me, very significant block of shares, Byron took a different tone. "This is an offering that people should run from as fast as possible," he wrote. "It's long on hype, drowning in red ink and dripping with inconsistencies and contradictory numbers." On October 25 the Wired IPO was soundly rejected by the marketplace. Wired's underwriters failed to take the company public even after cutting the price. The morning I learned that the IPO had failed, I stopped by the post office to make the minimum payment on my Visa card, and then I went in to the office to see if anybody was openly weeping.

I had often heard my brother say that it took real brains to figure out a way *not* to get rich if you were in the Internet industry in 1995, and I now had conclusive proof of my intelligence. In fact, by my brother's definition, I was practically a genius.

. . .

On the other hand, maybe I was in the wrong Internet business. E*Trade was challenging the discount brokerages via CompuServe, AOL, and the telephone, and its customers were mostly long-term or medium-term investors. But during the same years when Porter was building his online brokerage, a small number of outsiders were beating the market by scalping steady profits off hundreds of quickly executed trades. Although this early form of day trading has almost disappeared in real life, it lives on in the day trader's imagination. The people I consider day traders always take pains to inform me that they are not among those crazy gamblers who "scalp sixteenths."

It wasn't always crazy. Scalping sixteenths, or eighths, or even whole quarters of a point used to be a guaranteed source of free money. The chance first appeared after the crash of 1987, when the attention of federal regulators was focused on Nasdaq. Dealers on Nasdaq are supposed to make a market in Nasdaq stocks by taking the other side of customer orders. During the crash, the dealers had performed miserably.* Investors complained that they couldn't find anybody to buy the stocks they were desper-

---

* The Nasdaq market is "made" by competing broker-dealers who pledge to execute orders on both sides of the market. Ordinary retail customers never trade with one another. They sell to a market maker at the market maker's "bid" and buy from a market maker at the market maker's "ask." Profit for the market maker comes from several sources, including the "spread" between the bid and the ask; and speculative accumulation or sale of a stock based on the market maker's analysis of the price trend. The Nasdaq dealers benefit when the spread is wide.

ate to unload. The small investor without regulatory protection is at a huge disadvantage when the market starts to collapse, because the market maker simply has no incentive to buy a stock whose value is plummeting by the second. If there is nobody buying, the price drops even faster, everybody panics, and an old-fashioned debacle is at hand. The crash of '87 was not caused by a genuine economic meltdown but by a temporary institutional collapse. When the going got tough, the Nasdaq market makers hid under their desks.

The evaporation of liquidity during the '87 crash prompted a congressional investigation and some new rules. The National Association of Securities Dealers agreed that its members would participate in an electronic trading network devoted to small orders. The network is called the Small Order Execution System, or SOES (pronounced "sews"). SOES would automatically execute the order against the best posted quote. Even if market makers declined to pick up their phones, small investors would still be able to get in and out.

SOES was meant to provide protection for retail customers. Regulators expected most SOES orders to follow a defined path: an order would go from the retail investor to the broker, who would accept the order, to the market maker, who would automatically make the trade. Sometimes the broker would be a market maker in the stock, and the latter two steps would be combined. Nobody, apparently, anticipated that professional traders would use SOES to skim profits from their colleagues. These traders learned to take advantage of the system by watching their quote screens and waiting for the market to move against market makers who were slow in updating their quotes. They hit stale quotes for quick profits. The limit of 1000 shares per trade was easily skirted by making continuous small trades all day long, and by hiring additional staff to make additional trades. "I used to be able to execute two hundred round-trips per day," said one of the early SOES traders I spoke with. "It was like buying a can of Coke on one side of town for a dollar and selling it on the other side for a dollar thirty," said another. The SOES traders set up banks of desks where customers, after a modicum of training, could make their own trades.

This game was not popular with the National Association of Securities Dealers, whose members were getting hurt. Bigger brokerages had bigger and less controversial ways of making money, and they left SOES trading alone. It wasn't worth their while to antagonize their colleagues by searching out and hitting lagging quotes for 1000 to 5000 shares. But smaller brokers, especially those who disliked the big brokers, participated with gusto. Of particular annoyance was Harvey Houtkin. Houtkin was the first great SOES trader and for a decade the most vociferous SOES promoter. One weekend I met Mr. Houtkin in Southern California. "Every time I hit the machine my hands would shake," he recalled. The money was so easy it was embarrassing. "I had people who couldn't chew gum and tie their shoelaces who were making multiple six-figure incomes."

Houtkin's story is told in the arrogant yet self-mocking accent of Brooklyn. Although he is now a millionaire, he clings to the grievances of an outsider who learned the hard way that the really easy money on Wall Street would never be available to him. Houtkin grew up in Sheepshead Bay, where his father had a business in prosthetic limbs and braces. He went to Brooklyn Tech high school and then to City College, after which he tried and failed to break into the elite world of portfolio management on Wall Street. In Manhattan, Houtkin felt that he was viewed by his bosses as "City College scum." Undaunted, Houtkin started his own firm, only to see it vanish in the aftermath of the 1987 crash. Although the industry pulled together to make sure none of the biggest firms failed, some of the smaller brokerages were not so fortunate. "We had a major crash more severe than the crash of 1929 and not one major firm went out of business," Houtkin told me bitterly, "but I had four or five accounts with a big unsecured debit and I was allowed to fail. I lost my business and was treated very shabbily by the industry, and that's when I embraced SOES and started bringing it to the public."

This was sweet revenge. Market makers were losing millions of dollars to SOES because they were slow in updating their quotes. This had never been an issue before 1987, because the quotes in the regular Nasdaq system were basically advertisements that stock was available at a certain price.* Since actual buys and sells were made only when the market makers accepted them, traders had

* Offers to buy and sell stocks were posted by professional traders to Nasdaq's proprietary system, SelectNet.

some leeway to adjust prices or refuse the deal altogether if conditions appeared unfavorable. But SOES was an *automatic* system. If a market maker showed a high bid in a dropping market, he risked getting hit by a trader using SOES. It was only a few thousand shares at a time, but the mistakes added up.

"What came out of the 1987 crash," Houtkin boasted, "was a *virus*. I call it the Harvey virus." Houtkin's use of SOES was so aggressive, and his response to the National Association of Securities Dealers was so belligerent, that market administrators were seriously upset. "He's nuts," one regulator told the *New York Post*.

To make matters even more uncomfortable for the dealers, Houtkin publicly accused Nasdaq of deliberately maintaining inefficient markets so that insiders could take advantage of the public. By keeping the spreads large, dealers could buy low from a retail customer and immediately sell high to another retail customer. There was little risk that the dealers could be hurt by wide spreads, because the dealers could always negotiate directly for better prices on Instinet, which was a private network. Big traders who played by the rules would communicate by telephone and try to reach a mutually satisfactory agreement. In other words, dealers had access to better prices than customers did.

Sometimes it was even to the dealers' advantage to show a much higher quote than the rest of the market, because this justified selling to customers at this price, which would disappear when the dealer himself was ready to buy. The market was often out of line in this way in the morning, when changes in the European markets overnight had affected the American markets the next day. American dealers who delayed updating their quotes could trade advantageously against the public. With SOES, small-timers like Houtkin started jumping into the gap, and there was nothing dealers could do about it. "You are showing a thirty-seven bid?" explained Houtkin, pretending to press a button, "there you go." He smiled. "You are offering thirty-two? There you go." Thousands of dollars moved into Houtkin's pocket each time he pressed that button.

The market makers retaliated by dubbing Houtkin a "SOES bandit," and the NASD issued a series of rules that attempted to limit his use of the system. To the NASD, Houtkin was an unprincipled professional exploiting a technology meant only for retail customers. To Houtkin, the NASD was "the Gestapo" carrying out a "slash-and-burn campaign" that backfired. "They said we took advantage of them, but they would keep stocks artificially priced until they could do what they wanted to do with the public orders! Now, in the morning, every market is in line."

One day Houtkin learned—ironically, from a contact at the NASD—that on the Small Order Execution System he didn't even have to retype an order of 1000 shares (which was the upper limit per trade) if he wanted to execute it again. All he had to do was hit B and Enter. He demonstrated for me, alternately tapping his right and left index fingers on the desktop. He could buy 1000 shares five times in five seconds; this would cause the market makers to react by raising the price. "I'd be going like this"—tap, tap, tap—"and all the market makers would run like a pack of dogs. The stock would go up a half-point or a point then I'd hit sell and go like this"—more tapping. "It was a lot of fun."

The war was waged in the press, in arbitration hearings, and in the courts. The NASD pressured Houtkin's brokerage, and Houtkin accused the dealers of running a shamefully corrupt and unbalanced market. The truth was that market makers were unprepared for instantly executed orders; they were comfortable enough with the old system, where the big spreads made money plentiful. The SOES traders were irritants, but at first there weren't many of them, and the NASD was doing its best to end the use of the system by active traders. In a sense, the NASD's opposition to SOES trading worked to Houtkin's advantage, since it at first discouraged other traders from joining in the game.

Free money, however, inevitably attracts general interest, and by the early nineties there were dozens of shops dedicated to SOES trading. Many were run by small-timers and outsiders who had a beef with the National Association of Securities Dealers. Among the best of the SOES bandits was a very young trader named Jeffrey Citron, who had started as a clerk at Datek Securities, a small brokerage with a checkered past, when he was seventeen. By the time he was twenty, he and his friend Joshua Levine had written software to track Nasdaq prices and alert them when the market moved away from a stale quote so they could hit it via SOES. Using Citron and Levine's methods, Datek earned trading profits that ran into the tens of millions of dollars. Citron and Levine also made millions of dollars in sales of computer software and services to traders in other SOES rooms. Within a few years Citron was flying a Gulfstream jet and living on a majestic New Jersey estate he bought from a notorious penny-stock promoter named Robert E. Brennan.

One day Omar Amanat, who worked for Citron, heard a trader next to him at the brokerage ask why he couldn't make a quick electronic trade with other Datek traders without going through SelectNet—which was used by all the market makers, charged fees, and was slow. Josh Levine wrote software to enable intraoffice trading, and a new electronic communications network, called Island, was born. Because Datek was the leading SOES shop, Island quickly gained enough volume to be functional, and because the trades never had to bounce out of the system, they were very fast. While the volume didn't compare to that offered through SelectNet, traders found that their trades were executed often enough to make Island a good place to go for action in their favorite stocks.

With the creation of the Island ECN, Datek's trading environment was giving way to something new. It was no longer a matter of trying to beat the market makers using SOES, because market makers didn't go anywhere near Island. Island was similar to the "bucket shops" of the pre-Depression era, where gamblers bet with each other on the minute-by-minute moves on the ticker tape. Pre-Depression bucket shops were perfect for small speculators because they offered instant action. Traders could respond directly to prices, and they could take their profits or pay up their losses immediately at the cashier's window. Most traders lost, but some, such as the famous speculator Jesse Livermore, made money so consistently that they were banned from the bucket shops. (Livermore went on to become one of the great Wall Street players of the pre-Crash era.)

However, there was a crucial difference between the bucket shops and Island. The bucket shops were separated from the real exchanges by an impenetrable technological barrier. There were no mechanisms by which bucket shop "trades" could be traced or recorded on the exchanges, nor was actual share-ownership involved. They were merely gambling halls. Datek, by contrast, was a registered brokerage with legitimate access to Nasdaq, and the day traders using Island were the real owners of the stocks they bought and sold, if only for a few seconds. The electronic system at Datek was similar, in its basic structure, to SelectNet, the official NASD system. Traders who bought shares on Island could turn around and sell them, if they wanted, to Goldman Sachs or Merrill Lynch via SOES or SelectNet. Market makers could not see the bids and asks on Island, and this limited the system's liquidity; but this was an artificial, administrative barrier, maintained by the National Association of Securities Dealers to protect their profitable business.

. . .

The early nineties were the glory days of the day-trading shops, but the fun was about to end—or at least change. The fundamental guarantee of market-maker profits, which supported the whole antiquated system, was the large spread between the bid and the ask. In 1994, William Christie and Paul Schultz, writing in the *Journal of Finance,* exposed the fact that Nasdaq market makers seldom posted bids or asks for amounts other than whole dollars, halves, and quarters. Since quotes at odd-eighths—$\frac{1}{8}$, $\frac{3}{8}$, $\frac{5}{8}$, $\frac{7}{8}$—rarely appeared, the space between a bid and an ask was usually at least twenty-five cents, and often more. Customers who bought at the posted prices handed market makers a tasty profit on every trade. So lucrative were these wide spreads that big-volume market makers could actually pay brokerages to send them trades to execute. The broker would earn the commission fee, and the dealer would earn profit from the spread—kicking back part of this profit directly to the broker, with the customer none the wiser.

There was just one problem: a common understanding not to post odd-eighth quotes was a form of illegal price fixing, even if there were no formal agreements. The practice had gone on for years without challenge. But coming in the middle of the battle over SOES, the Christie and Shultz study shook the trading world. Richard G. Ketchum, the NASD's chief operating officer, called the Christie and Schultz exposé "irresponsible" and "slanderous."

Harvey Houtkin was overjoyed to see his enemies

squirm. He had argued for years that the SOES traders were merely delivering righteous punishment to big Nasdaq dealers who made fortunes ripping off the public with wide spreads and slow, squishy markets. Houtkin also knew from experience that market makers fixed the spreads, because whenever he posted bids or asks on a Nasdaq stock that were "inside the spread," he would immediately get harassing calls from the big brokerages telling him to cut it out. Now that the NASD was down, Houtkin hurried to add a few kicks. He talked with Scot Paltrow, a staff writer for the *Los Angeles Times,* and agreed to give him a demonstration of how price fixing worked. Sitting at his computer with Paltrow looking on, Houtkin entered a price for Intel that cut the spread to an eighth of a dollar. Here's part of what Paltrow saw:

> [Houtkin] punches in the symbol for Intel Corp., the computer chip maker that is Nasdaq's second-largest company. Houtkin, with 1,000 shares to sell, changes his posted prices. He cuts the "spread"—the gap between the best price at which any dealer will buy the stock and the price at which he will sell it—from a quarter of a point, or 25 cents a share, to a mere eighth of a point, or 12 1/2 cents.
>
> In response, a message flashes on his trading terminal from a much larger market maker, Weeden & Co.: "Pathetic."
>
> A caller who says he is Peter from Morgan Stanley complains: "You guys break the spread for 1,000 shares?"

Chiron Corp.'s stock has been trading with a 1/2-point spread; Houtkin narrows it to three-eighths. The phones ring again. This time, Keith Balter, head of over-the-counter trading at Weeden, tells Houtkin: "You're embarrassing and pathetic. . . . You're breaking the spreads for everybody."

Having the transcript of price-fixing calls appear in a national newspaper was bad enough, but the rest of the story was worse. In meticulous detail, Paltrow described the history of Nasdaq collusion, and the enormous, ongoing drain of customer funds. The reporter also revealed that the Justice Department had begun an investigation.

The *Los Angeles Times* story, along with the Christie and Schultz study, was part of a flood of bad publicity that was followed in the coming months by regulatory action. By the time the controversy settled, changes in Nasdaq regulations had unalterably transformed the market, putting an end to easy SOES money while opening up enormous new opportunities for retail traders. Nasdaq dealers paid almost a billion dollars in settlements and fines. More important, the Securities and Exchange Commission insisted that the National Association of Securities Dealers broaden access to their trading system, correctly predicting that more competition would decrease spreads. What did it mean to broaden access? It meant that Nasdaq would have to allow other electronic trading networks, such as Island, to link into their system.

Suddenly, the game was wide open. It had always been

possible to start an electronic communications network. Thanks to Datek customers, Island was thriving, and Reuters had created Instinet for the big institutional players. But the problem had always been liquidity. How could you generate enough orders to make a real market? Under the new rule, liquidity was guaranteed, because orders could flow back and forth between SelectNet—which the Nasdaq market makers used—and any number of private ECNs. Individuals could trade directly into the electronic system. The new rules were implemented on January 20, 1997. *Institutional Investor* magazine declared it Mayday II. After twenty-five years of delay, computers appeared to be on the verge of replacing traditional brokers.

Like Houtkin and Citron and other day-trading pioneers, Chicago stockbroker Jerry Putnam was something of an outsider. In the early nineties he was asked to leave Prudential Securities in a dispute over unauthorized trading. He formed a small new brokerage, called Terra Nova, with an ex–fighter pilot and ex–futures trader named Fane Lozman. Lozman had a patent on a trading screen interface called Scanshift, modeled on the cockpit displays of the planes he used to fly.

After reading some message-board posts in which Lozman claimed credit for helping launch the day-trading frenzy, I called him and asked him tell me his version of the story of how SOES trading morphed into the more widespread day-trading mania. Though we never met face to face, it was obvious after five minutes of conversation that Lozman, like Houtkin, came out of the marginal world of independent stock market operatives and small brokers who scalped uncertain profits without ever cracking through to the easy money. His stories were full of references to Chicago traders who "blew themselves out" with reckless plays in options and commodities, and of traders who had to move from one brokerage to another after their accounts got into trouble.

Lozman told me that his adventure in day trading began when he and Putnam were peddling trading software produced by Chicago-based Townsend Analytics to big institutional investors. This was a tough market, dominated by Reuter's Instinet and by Bloomberg terminals, which display information on stocks, bonds, and commodities, along with breaking news. "The problem with selling the Townsend software to institutions was that anybody at an institutional level realized that the software was junk. It kept crashing. It just wasn't a competitive platform." What Lozman was talking about was the first version of Real Tick, the trading platform that rescued me from the ambiguities of E*Trade. Over the years, he admitted, Real Tick has improved. "But you are still not going to go into any of the top hedge funds or banks and see a Real Tick platform," he said.

Lozman was being uncharitable. Real Tick, after all, was a Windows program. Windows was hardly the most reliable technology, especially in the early days, but it was ubiquitous among retail consumers. I asked one of

Real Tick's creators, Stuart Townsend, to see me. Stuart and his wife, MarrGwen Townsend, had a long history of building software for big financial institutions. How did they end up in the SOES business? "People were ordering more and more Real Tick terminals and nobody ever canceled," Townsend explained. He knew it wasn't the big banks that were buying them. Where were the customers coming from? He suspected they were the SOES traders. "We went to Terra Nova and asked Jerry Putnam to look into it. So Jerry went to Harvey's school."

Harvey Houtkin, bête noir of the NASD, showed Putnam the ropes, and the Townsends got busy marketing Real Tick to small-time players. That, at least, is Stuart Townsend's version of the story. Lozman says that selling Real Tick to day traders was his idea. "We took it to the trader who had maybe twenty thousand dollars in his account," Lozman explained. "Hey, it was better than reading off a tape, or CNBC." Lozman also introduced Putnam to notorious Chicago speculator Lewis Borsellino. With Borsellino and Townsend as partners, Putnam launched a day-trading firm that operated out of the Terra Nova offices.

A combination of insight and luck thus put Jerry Putnam at the center of the transformation of the brokerage industry. In 1996, when he examined the new trading rules that were being drafted in the wake of the price-fixing scandal, he was amazed by what he saw. Through competing ECNs, almost anybody would be able to display an order to buy or sell a Nasdaq-listed stock.

Putnam went to Stuart Townsend. "Do you know what this means?" he asked. Townsend understood perfectly. SOES money was peanuts compared to what was coming next. With the day-trading expertise of Terra Nova and the software skills of Townsend, a new, independent electronic communications network was created. They called it Archipelago, and it appears on my Real Tick screen as ARCA.

Why *Archipelago*? Because, buoyed by Datek's high volume of buy and sell orders, Island was the de facto leader in the ECN world. The name Archipelago was both a reference to the dominant competitor and a subtle pitch for what the Townsends believed was a superior, "open" technology. Orders routed to Archipelago automatically forward to other ECNs if they aren't filled inside the system. A nationwide, decentralized, transparent electronic market—and billions of dollars of new business—was being invented overnight. The trading prices tell part of the story. A fee of $20 for buying or selling 100 shares of stock had seemed revolutionary in 1994. Less than four years later, Tradescape, a new electronic brokerage founded by Omar Amanet, announced that they were pricing a 100-share trade at 1.50.

Neither Island nor Archipelago nor any of the seven other ECNs was dependent any longer on SOES scalpers. Attracted by the endless bull run, by SOES publicity, and by energetic marketing, legions of newcomers were arriving who thought they had a hunch about where the market was headed and who wanted the cheapest, fastest way to prove themselves right. By 1998 Island was trading 95 million shares a day, accounting for 10 percent of the volume in Nasdaq stocks. While much smaller, Archipelago attracted a $100 million investment from a group of the biggest names in the financial markets, including Goldman Sachs, Reuters Instinet, J. P. Morgan, CNBC, and E*Trade. Recently, Archipelago filed with the SEC to become a full-fledged stock exchange; this would allow them to easily trade stocks listed on the New York Stock Exchange, and Island is said to be preparing for the same move. The legions of electronic traders—retail and wholesale, amateur, professional, and institutional—are providing liquidity by interacting directly with each other.

"Why do you think the New York Stock Exchange and Nasdaq want to go public?" asks Harvey Houtkin, sarcastically. "To *bail out* on the public. This is the handwriting on the wall because they see the end. You'll be able to enter orders through an electronic mechanism, so what does the New York Stock Exchange do? Hmm, well, there's a lot of suckers out there; *we'll go public.*"

Stuart Townsend is, by nature, more measured in his speech, but he shares Houtkin's mission. He predicts that after some inevitable, heavily political battles, the ECNs are going to *be* the stock market.

The ex-small-time brokers from Brooklyn, New Jersey, and Chicago are positioning themselves to share the ownership of these new markets. They've realized that most breathtaking returns will not be in the trades but in the tools. This insight is not without precedent: San Francisco's streets are named not after gold miners but after the people who gave them a friendly word as they embarked toward the icy Sierra and sold them some blankets and a shovel.

Meanwhile, Fane Lozman is still pursuing his dream of a more ergonomic interface modeled on the cockpit of a fighter jet, and he haunts the story of the origin of day trading like an unwelcome ex-brother-in-law who inexplicably keeps showing up at family gatherings. Lozman split with Putnam long before Archipelago became a billion-dollar company. He complains that he was pushed out. Lozman resembles the Web producers of 1995 who believed they were staking a claim to the new Golcanda but ended up standing dazed on the sidelines as a mob rushed to the scene of a strike bigger than they ever expected. He still nurtures a faint hope that some of the new money really belongs to him. The last time we talked, he told me to watch the newspapers for word of his lawsuit against Jerry Putnam and the Townsends demanding his share of the loot.*

I learned two things from my foray into the history of day trading, one fuzzy and disconcerting, the other crystal clear and maddening. I learned that the mechanism of a trade was almost indecipherably complex. And I learned that E*Trade had been ripping me off.

* As this book went to press, I learned that his suit was dismissed.

I had naïvely imagined that E*Trade, as an electronic brokerage, arranged the sale and purchase of stocks between its customers and made its money from the commissions we paid on each trade. I suppose that if I'd been forced to describe a trade in more detail I would have guessed that when E*Trade didn't have an inventory of the shares I wanted to buy, it scooted out into the electronic marketplace, waved my money around, and acquired them for me. The price I saw was the best price anybody was willing to sell for. When I was ready to get rid of some stock, the price I received would be the best anybody was willing to pay.

This was not even close to correct. E*Trade never actually traded any stocks for me. Nor did it create some sort of electronic market through which I was communicating directly with other E*Traders. My E*Trade Web page was simply the front end to a traditional discount brokerage system. E*Trade did nothing but take my order on the Web and deliver me my confirmation on the Web. This eliminated a lot of customer service costs for E*Trade. But behind the curtain, it was business as usual. E*Trade sold my order to a market maker, who sold me the shares at his offering price and bought them back from me at the bid. Though spreads had narrowed, I still lost on every trade. A round-trip on 3000 shares of a stock that stayed flat but had a spread of $1/8$ cost me my E*Trade commission of $20 plus $375 in profits for the market maker, plus some other small fees—for a total cost of about $400. This might be good enough for an investor, but it was terrible for me.

Using a direct access brokerage and Real Tick, things made a lot more sense. In front of my face were all the players in the market. I could hit a posted bid or offer and pay the spread if I wanted, but I could also post bids and offers of my own and let other traders hit me. I could choose between routing my trade to a private ECN like Archipelago or Island, or I could send it to the Nasdaq market makers via SelectNet. It was all a matter of timing. And some hand-eye coordination. And something else. Some *magic*. Some *mojo*. Time and again, my trades were tangled in execution snafus.

One morning not long after I began using my new system, I noticed that a new issue had debuted. Oddly, it happened to be for a company I recognized, @Plan, which is pronounced "adplan" and has the Nasdaq symbol APLN. This online service tracks detailed demographics of visitors to Web sites and sells access to its demographic database to advertising firms and their clients. Unlike most of the companies whose stock I have owned, it offers a pretty good service, one that quickly became the industry standard. Every single one of the top twenty Web sites uses @Plan. But the IPO was received with somewhat less unanimous acclaim.

Maybe it was some temporary IPO doldrums, maybe people just didn't know the company; but either way, they weren't buying. APLN priced at 14, opened at somewhere around 15, dropped to 14, and made a lame run to a hair above 16. Which is the point where I started thinking special thoughts, thoughts indistinguishable from those of the people who should be my victims. "This is a darn good company," I said to myself, unconsciously adopting a hokey, just-up-from-the-dairy-farm accent. "At this price, it's a real bargain. If it starts to tank, I'll just hold on until the investors come to their senses. There's genuine value here."

The upshot of this arrant nonsense is that I broke a cardinal rule of successful day trading and jumped into an IPO on the first day. And that's when the cruelty started. Getting in was *easy.* Instinet showed 1000 at 16⅛ on the ask, and I took the whole offer. It looked like a good trade, and the price moved right up. For a second. Then Instinet came back with 1000 more shares. At 16¹⁄₁₆. Suddenly, it was like I'd awakened from a fit of sleepwalking that brought me down the steep staircase of the castle and out to the edge of the open drawbridge over the crocodile moat. What the hell was I doing here? I made to get out. As I plugged in a sell order at 16, I recalled seeing a warning come over the wire that SelectNet was down. Which was a problem because SelectNet was my best way of selling all 1000 shares to the market maker on the bid at 16. Maybe SNET is back up, I reassured myself as I pulled the trigger and entered a world of pain.

The sell order wasn't rejected. It just didn't go anywhere. Somewhere, perhaps on my broker's network, maybe on a Nasdaq server somewhere in New York, my order sat stalled in a frozen queue as I watched APLN dip below 16. My cancel orders went unaccepted. I tried to sell again, but since my last order was still pending, the automatic order-processing system assumed I was trying to go short. And you can't short an IPO. My new sell orders were rejected. Now APLN was at 15⅞.

Online brokers have backup customer service representatives sitting by the phone for just such emergencies as this. My broker picked up the phone on the second ring. I tried to explain the situation. He promised to check into it and call me back. Five minutes later APLN was at 15⅝. I called back, got somebody new, and tried to explain again. They transferred me to the trading desk, and I got disconnected. APLN made a leisurely retreat to 15⅜. Back on the phone, a third person listened to my story and asked me whether I wanted her to sell my position for me. "Well, I'd rather just have the thousand shares in my account, so I can sell them myself," I answered. I was still watching the screen. *Hello, 15⅛.* "But barring that," I added smoothly, "yes, I suppose you should sell, sell, SELL!"

Sold at 15¹⁄₁₆. The price tag for this three-minute fiasco: $1,053 plus commissions.

A few days later, I noticed an anomaly in my account. It looked like I was still playing APLN. More precisely, it looked like I was *short* 1000 shares of APLN. This meant I had sold the shares without owning them, giving me an obligation to buy them back in the future at my leisure. You usually can't short an IPO, which makes sense, since brokers like to open an IPO at a high price and sell lots of shares to the public during the first month, and then buy them back a while later, when sanity has reasserted itself.

It's wonderful to be short when the price is falling. APLN was down to 11 and change. I called my broker to double-check my status.

"Is my account short a thousand shares of APLN?"

"Yes it is."

"Well," I said, covering my delight with a slight cough. "I'd like to buy to cover." There is nothing easier than buying a stock that everybody hates.

"Done," she said.

The $4,000 I pocketed? I noted the profits in my journal as war reparations.

CHAPTER FIVE

TALKING POINTS

Day trading is lonely. Survivors tend to hunt in packs. All morning long, I've been surrounded by various simulations of community: the bantering heads on CNBC, Web discussion boards, multiple real-time chat sessions squeezing their way onto my screens. Of all the windows on my desktop, one takes precedence, because I've set it to remain permanently in the foreground: my Momentum Trader Internet Relay Chat (IRC) screen. Mtrader, as it's called, is where I get most of my ideas, where I do most of my socializing, and where my most trusted advisor gives court. Mtrader is the only window on my machine of which I read every single line.

That I'd be relying on a trusted advisor would have struck me as ludicrous when I first started trading. But then, I was never much good at predicting the future.

Back then, I had more than doubled my account size, and I entertained myself with visions of growing my low-six-figure trading account into a mid-six-figure trading account. Since I was trading the sum total of all the money I'd ever earned, borrowed, swindled, or inherited, this felt like quite an accomplishment. I gave myself extra points for having made a small fortune while the business page of the newspaper (which for the first time in my life I read religiously) was warning every day about the dangerous and unsupportable run-up in the prices of Internet stocks.

Sometimes I wondered if it was easier for me than for most people. I had a lot of tolerance for risk and seemed to have an uncanny knack for being at the right place at the right time. Even the technological mistakes were adding up in my favor. There's no denying that I had benefited from luck; but, on the other hand, perhaps luck is a talent like any other. You have to make the best of what you are given, I mused, and I seemed to have been given a gift for brilliant speculation.

During this time, a friend was regaling me with stories about the great money manager John Templeton, whom he had just met while researching a magazine story. Templeton, now in his nineties, had almost single-handedly invented the foreign-stock mutual fund. One of his earliest investors, Leroy Paslay, gave $65,500 to Templeton to invest in 1954, and by 1996 Paslay's shares were worth $37 million. The Templeton Growth Fund had an average annual return of 14.3 percent. "Templeton thinks stocks are overpriced," my friend told me, as if he were impart-

ing the secret code that unlocked the treasure chest of unlimited wealth.

I laughed out loud. Fourteen percent? You've got to be
kidding. In my first half-year of trading I'd made more
than 100 percent. The only times I went wrong were times
I strayed from the trading screen. In fact, I'd just returned
from a Christmas vacation that I'd been forced to cut short
when I'd seen that uBid, that great worthless IPO that had
been so profitable for me, had rocketed from around 35 to
more than 180 in the seven days I'd been separated from
my desk. If I'd only been trading over Christmas, instead
of traveling to see my mom, I'd have a 500 percent return.
I couldn't wait until the next morning, to find out what
new stocks to buy.

That conversation about Templeton, however, bore poi-
soned fruit, in the form of a 1932 reprint of a 1841 classic
about bull markets and their victims: *Extraordinary Popular Delusions and the Madness of Crowds,* by Charles
MacKay. MacKay's book was one of Templeton's favorites.
Since I was just beginning a reading binge about great
stock market speculators (in an effort to better understand
my heretofore undiscovered talent), I instantly found a
copy and started reading.

That day marked the end of my innocent triumphs. I
don't know what I expected. No, I do know. I expected a
friendly romp through the history of stock market dopes
whose bankruptcy would provide a suitably dark background against which the brighter stars of speculative adventure could be seen and appreciated. Today's deluded

losers, I was sure, were the dummies who kept saying the Internet was a fad and the Internet stocks were a joke. My bank account told me who was having the last laugh about that. I looked forward to a double handful of anecdotes about others who'd played the wrong runs, been plagued by the wrong timing, or been doomed by the wrong attitude—the better to torture my friends with. Although Templeton's returns were pretty weak by today's standards, he had been a player in his time, and I took it for granted that he would feel a kinship with me and my little victories over popular misunderstanding. If he was a fan of Charles MacKay, then I was prepared to be a fan, too.

The unexpected horror MacKay's tales inspired in me is hard to describe. Everybody knows about "tulipomania." The Dutch went mad about tulips a few hundred years ago and bid the price up outrageously—after which they came to their senses and the price fell. Big deal. Several hundred years later, their folly still lingers as the most trite of metaphors to be hauled out anytime someone thinks someone else is paying too much for something. Tulips are regularly mentioned on the stock discussion boards by desperate characters who are shorting a technology stock that continues, despite their evilest prayers, to go up and up. When I hear "tulip" I translate it this way: "I don't understand why this stock keeps rising but if it goes up another three points I'm going to be ruined." My response? "Tulip, you say? Time to buy more!"

So it wasn't MacKay's story of tulipomania that knocked me off my game, but his tale of the numerous

London bankruptcies in the wake of the South Sea bubble of 1720. Nearly everybody who touched the crappy shares of the South Sea company, with the exception of a few insiders, was damaged by the experience. Since MacKay tells it so well, there's no point in telling it again here. But the similarities to the run-up in the Internet stocks were terrifying. The advent (sometime in the future) of profitable trade with the Americas, which would transform the economy of England; why, that was e-commerce. The South Sea directors and their cronies, who sold their shares into successive waves of buying; these were the Internet stock-option millionaires. The manipulation of the price to ludicrous heights using publicity; this was the laughable "We're now an Internet company" press release. The proliferation of meaningless business ventures by London sharpies in the wake of the first great success, including "a company for carrying on an undertaking of great advantage, but nobody to know what it is"; why, this was uBid, and K-Tel, and Perfumania, and scores of others.

Explained MacKay: "It did not follow that all these people believed in the feasibility of the schemes to which they subscribed; it was enough for their purpose that their shares would . . . be soon raised to a premium, when they got rid of them with all expedition to the really credulous." *Hey, wait a second: that was me.* In the end, everybody went broke.

One dose of pessimism led to another. Soon I was devouring books about economic catastrophe. I read Charles Kindleberger's *Manias, Panics, and Crashes,* from which I learned that one sign of impending doom is the emergence of financial swindles that capitalize on the general belief that it is easy to get rich. Each day, my e-mail queue is peppered with announcements of new stock-picking services guaranteed to drown me with cash. In the past, I'd ignored them. Now, I saw them as omens of the rout to come.

Kindleberger even predicted the proximate cause of the latest phase of the bull run: the lowering of interest rates in late summer 1998, in response to the Asian crisis. The head of the Federal Reserve Bank, Alan Greenspan, had long been critical of the uncorrected boom in share prices, but when the Asian economies faltered he cut interest rates anyway, though this was likely to set off another manic stock market run to record highs—as it promptly did. Kindleberger, in his dry prose, writing long before the fact, reveals why even conservative bankers can't head off a dangerous bubble under these circumstances: "When commodity and asset markets move together, up or down, the direction of monetary policy is clear. But when a threatening boom in share prices or real estate or both rears up when commodity prices are stable or falling, the authorities face a dilemma." Indeed, they do. Greenspan chose a nice, easy rate cut, and I had $100,000 to show for it. For the first time, however, I began to reflect on the possibility that I would have all of this money stuck in a promising Internet stock on the very day that the market went south in a panic.

My fate was sealed when I settled down for the weekend with the ultimate stock market snuff movie: John

Kenneth Galbraith's *The Great Crash of 1929.* "The only reward to ownership in which the boomtime owner has an interest is the increase in values," Galbraith wrote. "Could the right to the increased values be somehow divorced from the other and now unimportant fruits of possession and also from as many as possible of the other burdens of ownership, this would be much welcomed by the speculator. Such an arrangement would enable him to concentrate on speculation which, after all, is the business of the speculator." This was an exact description of my heart's desire, but Galbraith's sympathy ended there. He seemed to take a cynic's delight in the fact that after the big drop in 1929 came the long, murderous compaction of the early thirties, by which point most of the amateur speculators had gotten all their funds pummeled out of them.

I had always assumed that even if the market dropped radically, all the traders in the world would simultaneously scream "buying opportunity!" and up we'd race again. I believed that after a big dip there would be lots of cash available to go back into the market. This, I learned, is a common misconception based on a failure to recognize that after a long, relentless bull run, a run that forces all the lingering skeptics to give in, *all the cash is already in the market.* And then it is gone. Gone where? Gone, as a great speculator once said, "where the woodbine twineth." He meant, I'm pretty sure, up the spout. Gone, in the words of another grim accountant, to join "the silent majority of vanished savings." In the Great Crash of 1929, stocks fell by 50 percent. During the next three years, they fell by another 80 percent. How were you supposed to make your money back under those circumstances?

Then and there, I concluded that my trading method was insane. Yes, I'd made a bundle of cash. But a circus chimp could have doubled his money buying the stocks I was playing during the winter of 1998–1999. It was simple. Dow hits 7,500 in August. Buy anything. Dow hits 10,000 by year end. Sell everything. Luckily, I was too dumb to know better than to get in at the bottom. But after dosing myself with MacKay and Kindleberger and Galbraith, I wasn't dumb enough to stay in at the top. I was finished trusting the market to reward me for not trying. It was time to trade risk for security.

My first task was to engineer a shift in attitude. When I'd started out, cashing in all my mutual funds and wiring the proceeds, along with all my savings, into my E*Trade account, I had made a conscious decision to trade it as if I were going to blow it. After all, I had just turned twenty-seven. I had a life of savings ahead of me. Might as well pull off all the risky investment stunts now, while I could still chalk it all up to youthful folly.

On the other hand, I don't think I really believed I'd lose it all. Perhaps "I don't care" was just a mantra to soothe the nausea and to quiet the panic that came late at night. In any case, now that I had had my payday—nay, my pay season—and was ready to double my stake again, I meditated on how I would feel if it were gone. Every few days, I tried on my old casual point of view to see if it still fit. "Easy come, easy go," I tried to say one night to my brother, but my voice trailed off into an anxious squeak. I'd done it. I no longer could convince myself I didn't care. If I lost it all now, I knew it would shape my identity for the rest of my life. I couldn't live with that.

Okay, the hard part was over. I'd admitted that I cared. Next, I needed a sensible trading strategy. I wanted rules. I wanted science.

In Edwin Lefevre's classic trader's travelogue, *Reminiscences of a Stock Operator,* the author recounts a conversation with a friend so unnerved by his investments that it literally keeps him awake at night. "I am carrying so much cotton that I can't sleep thinking about it," he told Lefevre. "It is wearing me out. What can I do?" Lefevre's reply was simplicity itself: "Sell down to the sleeping point." After spending the uncorrection of late 1998 bumbling into absurd profits, I thought I knew what my sleeping point was. It was zero percent stocks, one hundred percent U.S. dollars.

After all, who gets hurt when the music stops? The people who are still standing. The market equivalent of looking around in the sudden silence and realizing that all the chairs are taken is opening your trading account and staring at a list of securities whose value has fallen by 50 percent and is still dropping. If I was going to stay in the market, I wanted no risk of an overnight decimation. I was going to expose myself to the vicissitudes of the market for the briefest periods of time possible. My old mantra, "I don't care," was going to be replaced by a new one: "End the day in cash." That meant serious day trading.

I knew that my plan to reduce my risk by trading more often flew in the face of every investment commonplace. Nonetheless, the way I figured it, day trading was the *safest* possible strategy. After all, my favored Internet stocks had already risen 400, 500, even 1,000 percent. At this point, conventional wisdom was out the window. Buy and hold? The only person who held eBay all the way up was the guy who bought it at the IPO, went out for a bike ride, got hit by a car, and lay comatose in the hospital for the next three months.

No, now that the Dow had crossed 10,000, to buy and hold seemed laughable. I could just picture the big stock market managers, the traders for the mutual funds and the pension plans and the municipalities—for whom these new profitless Internet stocks had always seemed excessively risky—finally shaking their heads and capitulating. Every day I saw it on CNBC; the buy-and-hold crowd was getting in. It was time for me to get out.

If I was going to day-trade, I wasn't going to learn the ropes on my own. The issue of getting good executions was crucial if I was going to be making tens of trades each day. And although I was used to trading stocks I didn't believe in, and had even dabbled in stocks of companies that I'd never heard of, I was now going to be jumping in and out of completely obscure companies all day long. Where would I get my ideas?

Conveniently, the only thing the financial world offers more of than fools and suckers is experts. I found tip sheets promoted on Yahoo boards; guru Web sites with seemingly bulletproof track records; discussion board threads led by alpha traders; and any number of live chat rooms for the dedicated day trader. Some professed coherent trading philosophies, some just offered picks. Some of the leaders gave their names, some hid behind handles. Some sites were free, most had some membership fee. All looked bogus—except one.

A friend passed me the name: Ken Wolff. Wolff stood out in several ways. The most dramatic, least believable evidence for a trader's skill is an unverified record of successful trades, and there are countless Web sites that combine outrageously brilliant predictions with an invitation to join up for access to the next winner. This wasn't what I was looking for. Wolff's site, Momentum Trader (or mtrader), didn't list a single successful pick.

Not that he didn't brag; it's just that the self-praise on mtrader was devoted to the quality of the instruction in the rhythms of price oscillations on active stocks, rather than to yesterday's winners. I had already discovered, through my own impulsive experiments, that good and bad news moved stocks, with a quick but exploitable time delay. My challenge was to develop a method that was more powerful than sitting at the briefing.com Web page, which only gives you news of a stock's movement after the movement has already begun. I'd gotten lucky on Infonautics, but I wanted to be through with luck.

Wolff offered access to the mtrader chat room on a trial basis for free, and for $49 he sold me his instruction manual, *Momentum Investing.* As soon as I read it I realized I was in possession of a wonderful document. Wolff's firm belief is that "anyone of an average mentality and the ability to follow rules" can successfully make a living trading stocks. Unlike run-of-the-mill touts and charlatans, Wolff does not follow up this encouragement with vague and mystifying remarks about paradigm shifts or hidden gems. On the contrary, *Momentum Investing* has the matter-of-fact cynicism of the experienced sports gambler who tries to bet only when the odds are heavily in his favor.

I once met a knowledgeable Brooklyn horseplayer through some newspaper friends. "I only put money on two or three races per day," he told me, explaining that he looked for winners that the crowd overlooked. "The unexpected does not occur every race," he pointed out, "which is why they call it the unexpected."

This is Wolff's philosophy exactly. He is looking for the easy win, and using an iron discipline to stay away from all the rest. "I will patiently allow the market to bring a high-percentage trade to me and I generally make fewer trades than most day traders," he wrote. "I will allow many winners to slip away waiting for 'my' trade rather than to accept extra risk." To seal the matter, Wolff walks away from the trading screen at nine A.M. Pacific Time. He feels that after two and a half hours, all the bargains have been used up. Sometimes he returns to trade during the last half hour, trying to catch a breaking news story that will cause a stock to gap up the next day.

But it wasn't the techniques alone that captivated me, though *Momentum Investing* has plenty of straightforward advice about the minute-by-minute movement of the market. What I saw in the short manual, in Wolff's matter-of-fact cynicism, in his pragmatic willingness to drop any rule that outlived its usefulness, and in his easygoing faith in the democratic accessibility of wealth, was popular American small-business culture applied to the intricate working of the financial markets. If there was a sign that the Internet had changed things, this was it, for in Wolff's book there isn't a trace of the devil-may-care speculator, the sinister manipulator, the greedy scalper, the in-the-know insider, or any other old stereotype of the man who makes his money trading securities. In Wolff's world, a day trader who works hard and follows the rules is almost certain to make money, like any honest tradesman. (Wolff himself used to be a potter.)

Naturally, Wolff has a system. He believes that it is important to stay away from low-volume stocks, for instance, and from stocks with spreads of more than twenty-five cents between the bid and the ask. This is because a low-volume stock or a stock with bigger spread can move against you more quickly. You are betting that the price will go up or down, but you can also lose if the price stays the same, because of the spread. You want the stock, so you pay what is asked. Then you want out, so you sell for the price that was bid. Bingo—you lose the amount of the spread. The bigger the spread, the more risk you face each time you trade.

Wolff is cautious. He has the inherently conservative attitude toward capital preservation that any small-business owner has. Wolff advises taking profits at the first sign of weakness: a stock that goes from 11½ to 12½

and then back to 12¼ will be sold instantly to preserve
seventy-five-cent per share profit. Since Wolff's students
tend to buy shares in lots of 200 to 2000, this translates
into $150 to $1,500 in profit, and counts as a very successful trade. These are not big operators seeking a quick
million, nor are they manic SOES traders scalping market
makers for a quarter-point on 500 shares all day long.
These are people who—supposedly—are making two or
three successful trades each session and carefully accumulating their income, week by week.

Wolff's most valuable insights concern the patterns of
oscillations on stocks that are moving because of recent
good or bad news. The market always overreacts, he
teaches, and the way to win consistently is to buy on the
bounce at the bottom, or on the profit taking at the top.
Dumpers are stocks that sell off 20 percent or more on in-
significant bad news. As soon as the selling stops and the
buying begins, Wolff tips his students to join in for a little
upward movement as the market corrects itself. *Gainers*
are stocks that gap up 10 percent or more on positive
earnings or news. These stocks often sell off a bit at the
open, making them good short-term shorts, and then
climb, making them good short-term longs, and then fall
again, making them excellent short candidates after their
first high the next day. All morning long, Wolff watches
his screens, and tries to let his students know when the
selling has stopped and the movement has paused, and
then when new buying has begun. If you jump in when he
gives the word, you'll make a little money.

Sometimes, Wolff is wrong. And for small players rid-ing tiny price changes, a wrong call by the Jedi master can turn ugly fast. To protect his customers, Wolff stresses the importance of setting and sticking to "stops." A stop is a price, set in advance, that will get you out of a trade at a small loss. At sites like E*Trade, stops are easy to keep, since you can enter a "stop loss" order well in advance. The order informs the broker to get out of your position as soon as the price falls to a specified point. But for several reasons, stops are surprisingly difficult for Level II day traders to keep. For starters, you can't simply program your exit point in advance with software like Real Tick, since the burden of routing your order demands that you're present at the time of sale to decide between the available exit routes. Moreover, you are routing your own orders using the Internet. Network failure is one source of trauma; there are also times when distant troubles in the trading system foil your plans. Or you can simply make a mistake, trying to sell to a bunch of traders on a network where all the buying interest has disappeared. While you sit there deciding what the best way to sell might be, you lose time, and your rationality diminishes. It costs money to get in and out of a trade, so if you suspect the stock is about to move your way it is tempting to hold on for another moment and see if you can catch it on the uptick. This is the kind of spontaneous approach that results in bankruptcy.

I joined Wolff's online stock trading service, at a cost of $250 per month, and immediately I noticed people losing money by not keeping their stops. It was so obvious, so easy. Why were people failing? After trading hours ended one day, I drove up to Chico to meet the master. We had lunch on the patio of the Canyon Golf Club, above the putting green, where men in pink shirts were trying to end their afternoon with a successful putt before going in for an iced tea.

Wolff, who is about fifty, has a mellow demeanor and a philosophical attitude about people who can't keep stops. "Once a stock starts going down," he said, "how low is it going to go? I don't know. Nobody knows. So what happens when it falls through your stop, is you become emotional. First of all you say, 'Oh, gosh, I didn't stop. I'm down two hundred and fifty bucks. I should have hit it.' And by the time you say, 'I should have hit it,' you're down five hundred bucks. 'Oh, gosh, another five hundred. I can't stop out now because I'm down five hundred bucks. Oh, gosh, I'm down a thousand dollars now. God my wife's going to kill me. Oh, God. Oh, my God.' And by the time you say 'Oh, my God' for the second time you're down two grand. Then it becomes so painful, and it has happened so fast that you inevitably sell right at the bottom."

Wolff smiled. His description rang true to my own experience, except for the goshes.

Like many traders, Wolff got into the stock market by going long on a stock he had information about. This was pre-Internet; it was an oil company. He made a lot of money, and then lost it when the stock fell back. Unlike many traders, he spent the next months and years assiduously tracking his trading activity, taking notes and keeping a diary, looking for patterns, and making very small bets when he wanted to test a theory. He developed a great deal of confidence in his methods.

Wolff used to hang around the Shark Tank on AOL, watching Reverend Shark and other technical traders bait the buy-and-hold Gardner brothers. Wolff's entertainment was to bait the technical traders. "I thought everybody kind of knew everything I knew, and I found out very fast that nobody knew anything." Wolff would predict short-term price movements; for instance, he would announce that a certain stock that was being hyped by TokyoMex and others was likely to lose a half-point in the next few minutes. Since intraday price movements are easy to track, and Wolff's posts were time-stamped, it didn't take long for Wolff to gain fans.

At the urging of a few worshipful onlookers, Wolff agreed to teach his method of calling tops and bottoms to a group of a half-dozen or so would-be students, at a flat cost of $1,000 each. This turned out to be a big mistake.

"I went through hell. I found out that telling people when to make a trade is five times more stressful than trading. For one thing, I never blew a stop. I was too scared." This was not the case with his new students, who lost money and got angry. "I would say a stock is bottoming now at $20 and it is going to go to 22. Well, they would wait to buy at 20½ or even at 21 because they were still seeing some selling at 20. Then it drops down to close to 20 again. Now they're down three fourths because they bought so high off the bottom and they get so scared that they sell, and what do you know the darn thing goes back up to 21 and then right up to 22. Everybody is saying, 'Hey Ken, great trade,' but I've got several people who lost. They can't say much because I was right, but it was a killer for them emotionally. So after two months I quit. I said, 'That's it, gang, I taught you all I know, now it's free.' "

Wolff's idea was that he and his students would trade together in a real-time chat room. There would be no fee, just mutual support and assistance. Wolff would call a top or a bottom and then get back to his trading. When the stock hit his exit point, he would announce it and bail. Then, when the excitement passed, he would check in with his comrades.

Disappointment ensued. "I sell, I'm out, and I go back to the room and say, 'Hey, how are you guys doing? Wasn't that fun? I made a buck and a half. What did you make?' "

There would be no answer.

" 'Hello. Hi. Hey? Test, test.' "

Wolff was alone. His students were listening, but they weren't trading. Wolff discovered that to conduct a group trading session, even more explicit encouragement was necessary, along the lines of: "Okay, I see it dropping now. It's at 21⅛. This is not going to go below 20. See, it is still selling. Still selling. Still selling. Oh, here's some buying coming in. Look, we have buying. I would buy this right now at 20⅛. Buy it now. Now. Buy! Buy!"

When a couple of students offered to handle the technology and marketing side of the business, Wolff agreed to teach full-time. He has two hundred students paying $250 each per month. Since he can't effectively trade and handhold at the same time, he parcels out his trading account to his best students and they trade his money for him, following his calls.

Following Wolff's calls. There was the rub. I sat in the chat room and watched in awe. No doubt, his timing was uncanny, both in regard to individual stocks and in regard to the mood of the Nasdaq market generally. Once in a while I managed to take advantage of it.

During my first month trading in Wolff's room the market had a monumentally crappy open on fears that Brazil would be forced to devalue the *real*, with the country's Central Bank President Gustavo Franco resigning. S&P futures had the Dow down 150 points.

Five minutes after market open, briefing.com surveyed the damage:

YHOO –67 (–17%)
AMZN –34 (–21%)
BCST –72 (–32%)
CMGI –35 (–27%)
UBID –21 (–21%)
LCOS –24 (–23%)
DCLK –26 (–26%)
SEEK –21 (–25%)
GNET –17 (–17%)
NSOL –39 (–21%)

At the same instant, Wolff saw buying in the market, and along with all his students, I acted immediately to show him a bit more, jumping into a modest 500 shares of LCOS at 84. Less than an hour later, I sold my stake near 100. Eight thousand dollars, the easy way. Almost all the stocks briefing.com had listed as cratering were now in positive territory. I was glad I hadn't been holding any of them overnight, just another amateur investor who probably would've panicked and sold at the open. I was glad I was a day trader.

But usually I just sat and watched, unable to execute quickly enough as Ken made his calls. His method was easy enough to understand but very difficult to obey. At least my money wasn't completely wasted, because Wolff's room was populated by a cast of hilarious characters. There was Nesi, the part-time cab driver whose job was to scan a Dow Jones headline feed and post interesting news to the room as it broke. There was Threei, a mysterious and ultracautious Ukrainian master whose track record was so flawless some members refused to do anything but follow him. Dosty, who sat on the sidelines accumulating a stake with which to resume trading, seemed to haunt the room well into the midnight hours, spouting line after line of poetry, sometimes his own, more often Frost and Lawrence. Gimmie, an exceptional trader who eventually started and led an mtrader room for beginners, turned out to be Ken's daughter, supporting her two kids and husband by day-trading from Germany. Keeping order was the omnipresent Doc235, a sidelined trader and engineer who lingered on as a paid employee of Ken's, frequently and vigorously rebuking members who uttered anything that smacked of hype and cracking down on nonessential chatter with a schoolmarm's zealousness. It was clear that Wolff had cultivated some very successful pupils, a few of whom became co-instructors; their near psychic timing was evident for all to see.

Sometimes I wondered, though, how many of Ken's students were actually making money. Ken's advice to his students was to use his methods to identify their own stocks, and to treat his calls as an additional piece of data rather than as gospel. "Mtrader is not a stock-picking service," he warned on his Web site. "We strongly believe in teaching traders 'how to fish . . .' "

But fishing is tiresome, and if you happen to be standing next to a Long John Silver's and your stomach is growling, it's tempting to just drop in and order up a meal. Ken was severe in his warnings: "Follow someone else and you will be one of the many sheep at the bottom of a very steep cliff!" But I suspected that these warnings were unheeded, and that some of his students were frequently making leaps of faith off that cliff, one step behind their classmates.

One step behind is how I often felt in Ken's class. I'd be following Ken following the day's momentum movers— invariably some worthless also-ran that made me ill to just look at it—and I'd want to play, but I couldn't see the bottom. I'd be just a beat too slow. And by the time he called it, and I saw people playing it, it was too late. And then when I'd get stopped out—losing small, but losing—on something like Perfumania or Books-A-Million or Finet Holdings, I'd feel a creeping sense of shame that I'd ever owned even a tiny piece of such a dubious enterprise. I knew I wasn't supposed to be paying attention to that, and I tried not to, but sometimes I couldn't help it.

The more time I spent in the room, the more obvious it became that I wasn't the only one with problems. One day, a student I'll call Brantley piped up with this recommendation to buy Barnes & Noble (BKS): "Heads up folks: This is not the normal gainer or dumper play, but you probably want to check it out: I follow BKS closely, and have a position in it. They are spinning off barnesandnoble.com sometime very soon. It seems to be breaking out today, and is acting as if somebody knows the spinoff is very near. . . . I am gonna try to go long on the upcoming bounce if the pace looks good."

I was of the opinion that barnesandnoble.com, which would soon trade as BNBN, would be a hot IPO but a hard one to get into, and that people far stupider than I might pile into the flagship Barnes & Noble stock in anticipation of the spin-off. But I didn't particularly want to follow the trajectory of such nonsense mechanics on the message boards. It appeared that Brantley had done this work for me, so I took his advice and jumped into BKS at 37. As it turned out, there weren't as many people stupider than I as I had hoped, and I ended up selling the stock a day or two later for slightly less than I'd paid for it—which was fortunate, as it continued plunging from there.

It apparently didn't pay off for Brantley either. Nor did many of his other plays, as a few weeks later I found myself watching him in the chat room lament the decline of his grubstake. He announced that he had entered the room with $120,000 and was now down to $40,000. In the ensuing weeks, his posts got more and more frantic, woozy even, and he remarked that his "trading account just keeps slowly eroding away." Then he announced that he'd turned the corner and had made big money by changing his trading methods. "I gave up on the idea of following anyone else's lead," Brantley declared. "Thought for myself. Called my own plays. And, perhaps most importantly, I did my best to be as sensitive as possible, and to *listen* with my whole being. Then trusted the resulting instincts and the cues that made themselves known when I became still and silent."

"Are you smoking something, Brantley?" one student joked, but another, more experienced classmate had a serious comment: "I think one day does not a career make, Brantley. . . . after more time you will know."

A few weeks later, Brantley blew himself up in the ugliest of ways. It was a few hours into the trading day, and the room was watching CMGI, a holding company for various Internet stocks, and Priceline (PCLN), a "reverse-auction" site that sells airline tickets and hotel rooms. Brantley had entered into a long position on PCLN in the 130s, only to watch it drop sharply. Ken tried to call the bottom, and missed it several times. Rather than stop out and reenter, Brantley stuck with it all the way down. In the low 120s, he was out, and busted, and bitter. Sure enough, PCLN began to rise, and some other traders, who began to make money, complemented Ken on finally calling the bottom. "Anyone can guess a bottom on the fifth try, eh?" Brantley wrote. But the other traders were less than sympathetic. "I learned a long time ago no one is going to hold your hand, Brantley," was a typical comment.

It was easy to pick on a poor loser, which Brantley was, but I was afraid it would soon be me making nasty comments in the room after a stupid trade. There was a frustrating justice about Wolff's trading style, which demanded that you track the cycles of stocks with painstaking accuracy, and keep neat worksheets, and note the time of every trade, and write in your trading diary. The conservative, effective, shopkeeper style of planning segued instantly into heart-stopping risk and then back to rational, emotionless bookkeeping. There was money in it, but it wasn't easy money.

Maybe Wolff was right that you only had to be of average intelligence to master the system. But other qualities, rarer than intelligence, were called for. Could you add ¼ to ⁵⁄₁₆ without thinking? Could you lose, smile, and lose again, and smile again, and then put your money down for a third time on the same irritating stock, and then do it once more, all in the space of five minutes?

Could you look an elk in the face at twenty yards and string your arrow and shoot it through the heart without making a sound or jerking your hand? The elk is just a metaphor, but not a random one. After I became familiar with the demands of Wolff's trading system, I found it gratifying to learn that our teacher actually did hunt elk with a bow and arrow. This somehow underlined the fact that trading rationally required a peculiar constitution.

"When you're hunting," Ken told me, "you have to take into account many different variables, including wind direction, and how an animal behaves. You are very tense, and you are standing in readiness, but once it is time to perform, once you see the animal, the adrenaline hits your body, and you have to control that adrenaline and do everything that is reasonable to make the successful shot. My brother, it's funny, he just started day trading, and we've hunted together for years and he's an awful hunter. He's kind of like, 'Hey, look, Ken! There's a deer! Look! It's a big buck!' And at the same time he's said, 'Hey,' I've gone and shot the darn thing."

Ken says his brother is a good day trader, though. Ken keeps a close eye on him and tells him exactly when to buy and sell.

While watching and admiring Wolff, I continued to look for other promising trades. I noticed that others in the class did this, too. Sometimes I found myself following them. And sometimes I found myself at the bottom of a very steep cliff.

CHAPTER SIX

BIRDS
ON A WIRE

10 A.M. PST

Daytime television used to mean an afternoon of truancy and MTV, followed by a quick bustle around the living room to clean up the beer cans and burned matches before Mom came home. In the old days, daytime television advertising was a losers' gallery of correspondence courses and toupee'd personal injury lawyers. One thing that both the programming and the advertising took for granted was that anybody who was home on the couch at noon was willing to swallow some pretty hokey palaver.

This assumption is still valid. My day, as I've already mentioned, starts with a conversation between Mark Haines and Maria Bartiromo on CNBC. At four A.M., *Squawk Box* comes on. It's supposed to be a good show, but I can't really say; when the squawkers sign on, I am still struggling for a little shuteye. By five A.M. the TV is on, but I am not really paying attention. When *Market Watch* appears at seven A.M., I don't do much better, because by that point I am busy trading. For hours and hours, as the financial news continues, I zone in and out, noticing mainly that the ability of local sportscasters to improvise pseudo-interest out of the endless innings of an Oakland A's game has nothing on Bill Griffeth's talent for elaborating on the random walk of the Nasdaq market.

Hey, what's that sound? Dum, dum, de-dum, it's *Power Lunch*. Now *that's* my show. I wonder what's scheduled? CNBC has many theme songs, and they've all become fixtures of my consciousness. I love them. There's the simple four-note, the frilly builder, the rock-solo growler, and the staccato drone-on. I've been whistling the frilly builder all morning. I'm an excellent whistler.

Actually, I'm not such a great whistler; I'm merely loud. And I don't really love these tunes. I'm whistling them so loudly because I hate them. I'm whistling them *ironically,* because I really despise the fact that I've been listening to all the nonsense on this channel all morning, for the two-hundredth day in a row, instead of listening to a nice, relaxing Chet Baker album. The problem is, I can't stop. Without CNBC, I might miss something important, like the collapse of the *bhat,* or a surprise Greenspan dirge, or a Joe Kernen one-liner that could ruin my day. So instead I whistle, badly. I'm *butchering* the *Market Watch* theme song, and that gives me a tiny bit of lame satisfaction.

A question pops into my head. Am I working? After all, I'm certainly not relaxing. I push the question out of my head quickly, with the help of my piercing whistle, because it is past ten now, and it is time to get over my ambivalence and start paying attention.

This is the middle of the trading day, the time when day traders get depressed and attempt to "force" the market—and lose money. There are bars in my neighborhood that are more active than the market at midday. (Well, there *were* bars, until recently; most have been closed or converted into bagel shops, Starbucks outlets, and lofts.) Predictable moves are hard to find, and like everybody else I'm looking for a few magic words on CNBC that'll create a little action. Over at mtrader, Ken Wolff has signed off already, taking a break before the last half-hour of trading, and Doc235, his able assistant, is warning newer players about the midday dead zone, the Bermuda Triangle into which a momentum player's entire life savings can vanish, never to be seen again. Doc addresses us placidly. "Newer traders and trial members," he writes, "we are in a time period we consider to be low-percentage trading. We usually see pace decrease as we move into afternoon trading so we need to be careful. . . . Wait for quick moves in stocks or for news plays that can warrant a trade." To me, the important words Doc utters are "news plays." I made my first real day-trading money from briefing.com, and still have a soft spot in my heart for the quick scalp off a headline.

Where are those headlines going to come from? More likely than not, the good tidings will waft from the lips of Joe Kernen, the gap-toothed CNBC stocks editor whose *Winners and Losers* segment has made a few fortunes.

I want Joe, but I'll take anyone. In my personal history

of immaculate trades, the ones I most cherish are the ones that stemmed from some breaking news item on CNBC. The best-case scenario is when you already know what they're going to say before they say it. Very little of CNBC's reporting is original, and if you're watching the Dow Jones wire closely you'll know most of the good news as it unravels. But if you have failed to become expert at felling elk with a bow and arrow, you'll hesitate to play a Dow Jones story at the moment it hits the wire. In fact, this will probably be the very moment where your consciousness of your own ignorance hits the high-water mark. You'll see the story but it takes a minute—a crucial minute—to figure out whether it is good news or bad news. You'll wait to see volume picking up, or a briefing.com mention, or an uptick in the price, or some other obvious event that clears the matter up—and then you'll know it's far too late to get in. On the other hand, if you hear CNBC rolling into a news mention of the same stock a few minutes later, you almost can't lose.

A few months ago, the chairman of my favorite Internet holding company, CMGI, came out and announced he'd be opposing the USA Network/Lycos merger that had been advocated by Bob Davis, the Lycos CEO. Since CMGI was a major Lycos shareholder, this was bad news for the merger, but good news for the Lycos stock.* When the

---

* In this case, I knew the back story. USA Network, a home shopping channel run by Barry Diller, had an established business that could be valued based on the traditional ratio of earnings to share price. Lycos, on the other hand, was an Internet portal; in fact it was the very Internet portal that bought Wired Digital, including my site, Suck. Because USA Network was a real company doing

merger snafu hit the Dow Jones news wire, I put LCOS in a Level II window. When David Faber opened his mouth to repeat the news a few minutes later, I was in for 1000 shares. When he closed his mouth, I sold the stock, for a profit of 3 dollars per share. Five seconds later, as the market digested the CMGI executive's remarks and realized that it would take some serious unraveling to sink the deal, LCOS was back down to where it started, but I wasn't. I was richer. And I was happier. And I was grateful to CNBC.

Another good CNBC play was to check the CNBC Web site and write down the schedule of CEO appearances. You lined up their companies in your trading windows, and as each executive came on you went short. The CEO appearance was, dollar for dollar, the most reliable nonnews event the stock market had to offer, because hope sprang eternal amongst the inside-angle-searching E*Traders, who usually managed to convince themselves that Mr. CEO, the head of some company they'd been foolhardily accumulating for months, was finally ready to announce a gigantic buy-out, or earth-shattering earnings, or a mega-investment-cum-beatification courtesy of Pope

---

real business, its stock was earthbound by real economics. Since Lycos was an Internet business that would make huge amounts of money in the future, its stock price could go as high as infinity. Therefore, a merger of USA Network and Lycos was a bad deal for Lycos shareholders like CMGI. It turned their high-flying speculative Internet company into a regular old profit-oriented company. The deal was obviously a bonehead play, and in fact Lycos shares tumbled more than 50 percent in the following weeks. If the merger was off, then the risk that Lycos stock would be handicapped by old-fashioned valuation models was off, and the sky was once again the limit.

Gates. Reliably, this did not happen. Important news was never released by surprise in CNBC interviews with CEOs, at least never when I was watching. Instead, the boss repeated old news, joked lamely with the interviewer, and answered "hard" questions with the exact same sentence the company had been using for weeks. The E*Tards, who had grabbed just a bit more stock in anticipation of the televised chat, quickly reconsidered their strategy. In other words, they bailed. A little bailing led to a little more bailing, and in the few minutes before the market recovered there were usually a few pieces of bacon available for snarfing by the cynics in the crowd.

This is good stuff, but it isn't for me, at least not today. The troubling fact is that I have grown concerned about my executions, and playing "short-the-CEO" calls for slightly better timing than I was confident I could achieve. Sometimes, you see, the shorts started shorting before the CEO actually appeared; then when he started talking they would buy to cover, and the price would counterintuitively (or is that countercounterintuitively?) *rise* as he released his preprogrammed pleasantries, and I would get a half-point haircut. To deal with this you had to be able to get out quickly, and I have been getting caught too often lately with my finger on the trigger and a little drop of spittle on the edge of my paralyzed lip.

Instead of playing, I am watching. Mostly, I am watching the commercials. There is nothing that can restore the faith of a day trader faster than a series of commercials for online brokerages. However, the reason for this is not what the chairman of the Securities and Exchange Commission, Arthur Levitt, thinks it is. Not long ago Levitt took aim at some of my favorite ads, saying they encouraged novice investors to make irresponsible bets in the stock market. A great advertisement for Discover Brokerage—one that really got the chairman's back up—shows a big-bellied tow-truck driver poking down a rural highway, having rescued a condescending business executive who sits in his shirtsleeves in the passenger seat. The executive looks down and sees a copy of *Barron's,* and reveals with a subtle movement of his face that he finds the juxtaposition to be humorous.

"You read *Barron's?*" asks the suit.

"Oh, yeah, all the time," answers the tow-truck driver, who explains how *Barron's* has rated his favorite online broker—that's Discover, natch—as the best of the bunch. The suit is even more amused.

"You, ah, invest online?"

"Oh yeah, big time. Well, the last few years anyway. I'm retired now."

"You're retired?"

"I don't need to do this. I just like helping people."

Disconcerted, the suit looks up and notices a picture postcard. "Vacation spot?" he asks.

"Actually, it's a picture of my house."

"But that's an island."

"Well, technically, it's a country," says the driver, then bang, we're out, the hard-driving beat leaving us with the white-and-red-on-black cue: Discovery Brokerage. But wait, we're back. "Weird thing about a country, though," adds the driver. "You've got to name it."

And now we're really out. "Woowee—go get 'em, cowboy," I muttered, every time I saw it.

For obvious reasons Chairman Levitt was skeptical about this ad. "In today's bull market, there *may* be an increasing population of tow-truck drivers who now own their own islands as a result of online investing," he said sarcastically during a speech to the National Press Club. The chairman even called the advertisers into a private conclave to encourage them to set some guidelines that would limit the claims they could make. I talked to a couple of people who had been present at the meeting and I found, to my relief, that they were not cowed.

One of the attendees was John Yost, a founding partner of Black Rocket, the San Francisco agency that produced the Discover ads. One day, when the market was extremely dull, I walked over to his office at Pier 33. Yost projected a serene sincerity when he talked about the way he expects people to respond to the appealing tow-truck driver and his private island home. "People want their messages wrapped up in some baloney so they can digest them more easily," he said. "They understand that advertising is hyperbole and exaggeration."

Above Yost's head, taped to the conference room windows and walls, were ads that his company had produced for Yahoo. Several pitched Yahoo's finance section, which offers stock quotes and investment analysis along with the infamous discussion boards where the rabble go to hype and be hyped. In one of the ads, a pair of nuns are splashing joyously in the ocean. Next to the words "Yahoo Finance," the caption describes the thrill of having gotten out of the market just before it crashed. In another, a young girl sits on her bed and writes in a book, "Dear Diary: Today I found out I'm worth more than my parents."

In many of the Discover ads, the young, the old, the working-class, and the humorously freakish triumph over today's universal enemy, the middle-aged Caucasian man in a business suit. For instance, a taxi driver refuses to allow a pair of corporate parasites to take over a company whose financials aren't good enough. "If you are going to do a hostile takeover from my cab," he says, "do one that's more worthwhile." A pint-size longhair steps in front of a craggy executive and into a Rolls-Royce towing a yacht. "Do you need a lift somewhere?" he asks. A teenager confronts his angry father, who takes away his Discover privileges because he was out too late. Heading out to the lawn where his personal helicopter is idling, the son cries bitterly, "You can't control me forever!"

The online brokerage business, Yost pointed out, is a blow for democracy. "The stereotypes that have been used to define successful investors are irrelevant. Farmers and school teachers and plumbers are taking responsibility for their own investments. If you really care about your health you have to be more involved in learning about medical care; if you really care about your financial health you have to be more involved in investing your own money."

Other brokerages strike exactly the same note. E*Trade has attacked the traditional brokers, portraying them as selfish slime who would push you into worthless stocks for their own benefit.* Ameritrade dissed the lazy investors who stuck their money in mutual funds. The lesson of all the ads, taken together—and on CNBC they play in constant rotation—isn't really that you can become a gazillionaire. That is merely an exaggeration to make a point. The lesson is that by playing the market in a savvy and engaged manner you can kick the stuffing out of index funds through well-timed trades and superior research. The lesson is no different, at core, than the lesson of Peter Lynch, or the Motley Fools.

The lesson is very important to me. I, too, consider the middle-aged Caucasian man in a business suit to be my enemy, and I do not underestimate him. That man—the man who really controlled the stock market during its pre-Internet phase—was a professional money manager, banker, or stockbroker. He may have been slimy, or he may have been a model of rectitude and community service. He may have subjected his investors to a random walk toward bankruptcy, or he may have given them a nice consistent premium over the index funds, or he may have merely sold them an index fund. But whatever he

---

* This approach was not open to Discover, since Discover is owned by Morgan Stanley Dean Witter, which still employs whole villages of stockbrokers.

was, and whatever he did, chances are that he had access to better tools and more information than I did. As long as there was an inside, and I wasn't in it, playing the stock market was a dangerous game. But now, as Discover never tired of pointing out, even rural pig farmers are on the inside, which meant there isn't an inside. It is come one, come all, the water's fine, and the devil take the hindmost. With the entire population of North America involved, well, that changed the odds substantially. No insult to my fellow citizens is intended, and I hope none is felt. They would be right to think the same comforting thought about me. The less the market resembles a private club, the less likely it is that I am the Greater Fool. Fidelity's advertisement put it with great eloquence: "When the bulls start running, you can bum a ride."

CHAPTER SEVEN

THE
MIDDAY
STRETCH

12:00 P.M. PST

It's exactly noon and there are no news trades that I am willing to go out on a limb for. This has been happening more and more lately. When I hear a piece of news that seems good for a few points—a settled lawsuit, for instance, or a deal to put a front-page icon on Yahoo—I worry about whether this isn't actually new news at all. Haven't there been rumors to this effect already? What if all the impact is already priced into the stock? And then my execution anxiety takes hold, and I wait to see what happens. It is always safe to wait. You never lose any money waiting.

Maybe I can find a nice range-bound oscillator. I've never lost the habit of looking for slow, easy position trades like the ones that had wined me and dined me in my E*Trade days. If you can find a company with strong support, you can play it up and down as it gently undulates—while waiting for a good pop when the whole sector moves.

One week, I played Oracle, which I knew was a key company for Internet commerce, for four days straight. Two thousand shares a whack. Oracle was low-maintenance stock, something I could play in the background while more volatile day trades occupied my foreground attention. The first and second days were just scalps, sixteenth-points one way or the other. The big shares I was playing—big by my standards, as I hadn't yet started having the $100,000 days I felt sure would come eventually—made me nervous and spooked me out of trades too soon. But I'd been watching Oracle and playing it, and with watching and playing comes learning. Pretty soon I was tuned in to its wavelength. This one would make me some real dough if I cracked its code. So I did.

Attempting to crack the code is a favorite hobby of the amateur trader, and it infects professionals, too. Every time more data about stock movement have become available, the applied science of technical trading has seen progress. Long-Term Capital Management, a billion-dollar hedge fund, was the advance guard of this progress. Their infernal machine, designed to take advantage of complicated relationships in the options market, blew up when the Asian crisis hit in 1998, taking major pieces of flesh out of several upstanding citizens of the investment community. Only a timely corporate bailout, encouraged by the Federal Reserve Bank, saved the day.

The high-level mathematics and computerized trading models that allowed the Ph.D.'s at Long Term Capital to bankrupt their billion-dollar hedge fund were not available to me, so I was using simpler methods. The key was to recognize the regular pattern of small, up-and-down movements, and ride the waves. Just as online brokerages brought the tools of the broker-dealer into the living rooms of ordinary people, the relentlessly compounding increases in computer processing power made it possible for me to receive timely notification of stock movements.

The tool that most beautifully embodied my dream of automatic profit was a Web-based technical analysis site called ClearStation. ClearStation's inventor, Doug Fairclough, is an ex-colleague of mine from Wired, and his apartment is barely three blocks away from mine. It's time for my Starbucks anyway, and since the midday market is going nowhere, I make a short detour on my way to the corner and go to see Doug.

As a demonstration of faith in his device, Doug sleeps until noon. All his trades are programmed in the night before. "You know Xanax?" he asks me, standing shirtless and bleary-eyed in the doorway after ignoring for ten minutes my violent pounding on his door. I admit that yes, I do know Xanax. There is a whole shelf of my medicine cabinet devoted to anti-anxiety drugs. Doug shrugs. "Well, that's the story," he explains.

ClearStation is now owned by E*Trade, which bought Doug's company for a pile of stock. ClearStation allows users to create complicated technical charts of stock movements on the Web, for free. You can graph the fifty-day moving average using ClearStation. You can annotate your histograms and your stochastics. You can count your money. E*Trade, having recognized that active traders like me are good for huge piles of commissions, has gotten in the shovel-selling business.

Although Doug's company is owned by E*Trade, he is not required to go to work at their offices. This is undoubtedly a good thing, I think to myself, because Doug would not fit well in a corporate environment. Even at Wired, which had a high tolerance for idiosyncrasy, Doug irritated his bosses. I remember seeing the company's chief operating officer stand up at her desk one day, stare calmly across the room to where Doug was supposed to be sitting (it was still before noon), and say, stressing each syllable, "I am going to fire him."

Today, the most lived-in part of Doug's apartment is a basement rec room, which contains a large pool table covered with outdated newspapers and magazines. A string of blinking white Christmas lights wanders around the walls, and there is a three-foot by five-foot wooden desk whose edges are marked by burns from cigarettes fired up and forgotten during late-night hours. *Hey, wait a second, That's my desk. I loaned Doug that desk. And now it's all burned.* Oh well; if I learn how to use ClearStation properly maybe I can set its dial to "a million dollars" and buy as many big desks as I want.

Doug is interested in my package of Nicorette. "Does that stuff work?" he asks.

"Yep," I answer, "but now I'm massively addicted to the gum."

"Maybe your lungs will clear up though," says Doug, who has a cough.

Doug lined up his trades last night at four A.M., and hasn't looked at the market since. "The less you can look at what the market is doing the better off you are," he says, "because the market is very distracting."*

Doug has already gone broke twice trading stocks, but that was before he had his system. The first time was in 1987 when the stock market fell 500 points. Doug called his broker and found out that he'd had a margin call and that all of his stocks had been liquidated to pay off the debt. He was very upset. In 1991, when he had built his savings back up to about $40,000, he went broke again taking oversize options positions. Like all dedicated traders, Doug values these traumatic experiences as a form of tuition. (Even the serene Ken Wolff has told me, with relish, about being "curled up on the couch with flu-like symptoms" after a painful loss.)

Before the '87 crash, Doug's approach was to buy fast-moving stocks, and then flip into other stocks he thought were moving faster. "This is a common way people trade today," he says ruefully, "and it is incredibly hard to do

---

* In fact, Doug told me later that his Xanax is not for trading anxiety. "Why get anxious if you know what the market is going to do?" he said. "Note that I was trading by day and blasting out new ClearStation features by night, sometimes going days without sleep. The odd thing was that instead of getting tired I'd be more and more keyed up until Señor Xanax had to stop by."

because you get into this syndrome of saying, 'Well, this one's not moving enough, I'm going to sell and jump into the other one.' Right then the other one stops moving and you jump back into the first one." Doug gets a faraway look in his eyes. "You know," he adds, "every time that happens, chunks of your body are being hacked off. After the crash I just drank pretty heavily because it was a couple of years' worth of saving that had evaporated."

Doug's mental-health goal is to stay emotionally uninvolved in his trades and not get elated when he wins or depressed when he loses. "I've definitely mastered the part about not feeling elated," he reports, "but when things go down and move against you, that's something I haven't yet mastered."

Since ClearStation automates a lot of the stock-picking drudgery, it allows Doug to reduce his emotional vulnerability. After his first two experiences with losing everything, he is especially skeptical of the value of CNBC. "I was sitting in front of CNBC every day and that was a disaster because it would suck me into being reactive to each fluctuation and I didn't have a bigger picture, or even a chart. There weren't really any PC-based charting systems that I could use then, and if you are going to do any type of technical trading you at least need to see a few variables charted over specific time frames."

The basic dimensions of technical analysis are price and volume, but since the market is dynamic these variables need to be measured in time; this gives rise to second-order variables such as the moving average and the rate of change, and then to additional, ever ramifying graphs and equations whose goal is to establish the levels of support and resistance. *Resistance* is the level beyond which a stock's price is unlikely to rise without significant good news; *support* is the level beyond which the price is unlikely to drop without significant bad news.

To value-oriented investors, who place their faith in the actual business a company does or doesn't do, technical variables like these are so much hocus-pocus. Since financial facts—both micro and macro—account for value, you can expect stocks to make only small, random deviations from their fair value. Calling the upper and lower boundaries of these deviations resistance and support is giving occult significance to a statistical by-product.

But to technical traders like Doug, the concepts of support and resistance are simply common sense, partially quantified. Say a heavily traded stock called XPOS has risen to 90 and then fallen back to trade in the mid-80s. Now 90 will represent a level of resistance, because a significant number of shareholders bought the stock as it approached 90, and then they lost money. Even shareholders who bought the stock lower will have mentally tallied their profits when it hit 90 and will now believe themselves to be losers of some of these "paper profits." A feeling develops that 90 is as good as it gets. Therefore, as the stock approaches 90 again, shareholders will take the opportunity to make good on their losses or take their profits, such as they are, and sell, driving the price down. After a couple of swings like this, it becomes ingrained in the collective memory of the market that XPOS doesn't like to go above 90. Traders will consider 90 a natural limit on the price of the stock, absent good news. Resistance becomes a self-fulfilling prophecy; people believe it because it works, and it works because they believe it. Once the stock breaks through 90, though, all bets are off, and now new people—or even some of the people who sold at 90—will jump in; after a few oscillations, the stock will establish its new trading range. The concept of resistance makes sense of an otherwise irrational policy that technical traders have: they avoid stocks until they have "broken through" the resistance. In other words, as the price goes up, the stock looks like a better deal. Value investors, it goes without saying, consider this the height of lunacy.

After going broke twice, Doug wanted to give himself better odds, and he began to carefully chart the movements of stocks he wanted to trade. Since Doug was a database programmer, it seemed obvious to him that this should be done via computer. He wasn't a professional trader, and he didn't want to pay hundreds or thousands of dollars for professional-level trading tools, such as a Bloomberg terminal. He wanted to get his data from the Web, for as close to free as possible. So he bought a CD-ROM that contained stock and mutual find prices back to 1982, and then he wrote a program to automatically extract updates from a popular Web site and post them on his own site. From this raw material, he starting building the tools to allow him to automatically see the moving averages along with more esoteric figurations such as the histogram and the stochastic. "It's not just predicting the future from reading tea leaves," chortled one value-oriented analyst I know, upon seeing ClearStation for the first time. "It's predicting the future by doing *chemical analysis* of tea leaves!"

But in this long bull market, it's been working pretty well for Doug. For one thing, it helps him keep track of more stocks.

"It's just hard to have a persistent picture of what happened last week, you know," Doug says. "I have the computer do as much as possible because there are thirty thousand securities out there."

But even more important is the ability of ClearStation to keep Doug away from the trading screen. "The more time I spend watching real-time quotes and seeing what my positions are doing, the more likely I am to do something stupid. The market is such a whirl of emotion, there are very few people who can stand up to it and not have their judgments influenced by all the activity." By using ClearStation to track the stocks that have momentum, Doug's been able to shift from the online brokerages and auction sites, which ran up in the fall, to the broadband companies, which ran up in the winter, to the hardware companies, which started running more recently. All these companies are high tech, all are part of the Internet boom, and all are valued at levels so astoundingly high that nobody but a madman, an ignoramus, or a technical trader would go near them.

"But Doug," I ask, following the thread of my ongoing investigation, "why do so much work on the business side of ClearStation if you can just make money trading?"

"I am going for the big kill," Doug answers. "I saw that the commercial opportunity for ClearStation was greater than the amount of money I could make using it to trade." Doug blinks his eyes and yawns. "But, yeah, I mean my personality is more suited toward trading than, you know, running a company."

I look at the clock. It is now ten minutes before one. If I am lucky and the baristas at Starbucks are sufficiently bewildered by my order for a triple-double, I won't make it back to my loft until just after the market closes. I take my time walking to the coffee shop and then home.

The elevator in my building automatically returns to the ground floor after every use, so it is waiting for me as I enter the lobby. This could mean trouble, but fortunately it's a slow elevator. I get off on my floor and walk without hurry down the hall. I turn my key deliberately. I enter. The television is still on. Then I hear it—*ding, ding, ding.* The market is closed.

I exhale with relief. I am afraid of one o'clock. Doug was right. The more you look, the stupider you get, and the end of the market day, with its last-minute volume swells and its irresistible promises of a gap-up in the morning, has lured me into some of the more disastrous trades in my short career. There are seventeen and a half hours between one day's close and the next day's open, and that is a long, long time to be on your knees, hands clenched tightly, looking up at your twenty-four-foot ceiling, praying that if there is a God, he isn't just.

When there is significant news at the end of the day, the risk is increased. News plays are among the most difficult to make successfully at the close, for the simple reason that where there is news, there is always the possibility of more news, which proves that the first news wasn't really news but rather hype, or rumor, or even a spelling error, as may have happened when stock in Juniper Group (JUNI) rose inexplicably during a bull run on Internet hardware firms including Juniper Networks (JNPR). Stocks played by day traders are especially vulnerable to sudden reversal, because the rush to beat the crowd often prevents anything but a quick skim of the press release that contains the wealth-creating revelation.

Take EntreMed. In May 1998, *The New York Times* carried an enthusiastic report about two cancer-fighting agents, called angiostatin and endostatin, developed by Harvard scientist Judah Folkman. The rights to develop and sell the drug were owned by EntreMed, a Maryland biotech company. Several years earlier EntreMed had signed a well-publicized partnership agreement with pharmaceutical giant Bristol-Meyers. In the wake of the Bristol-Meyers deal, EntreMed went public, and their stock (symbol ENMD) was trading in the 10-to-15 range. Then the *New York Times* article appeared, and the stock immediately went to 85, in the speculator's fantasy scenario: Small Biotech Company Cures Cancer. Cooler heads soon prevailed, and the stock price fell back to about 30. But it remained volatile, running up and down on various announcements of progress or setbacks. This is normal for small biotech companies who depend on a few drugs for their success, and during the fall and early winter I completely ignored the story.

Then came Armageddon. Bristol-Meyers announced they couldn't reliably produce angiostatin and endostatin and were dropping their development of the drugs in favor of more promising compounds. EntreMed, which had faded to about 25, promptly collapsed, shedding half its value overnight. The market had spoken, dealing out corporal punishment to the longs, gold stars and hall passes to the shorts, and nothing, yet, to me, as I only became aware of the hullabaloo when the time to take advantage had passed.

Or maybe not. A few days later, with an hour to go in the session, the Dow Jones news wire picked up a *Boston Globe* report that the National Cancer Institute had duplicated the good doctor Folkman's results. Tumors in mice had shrunk. Permission was sought to begin testing on humans. Cancer was practically cured, and I was one of the first to know. This was a no-brainer, and I bought some EntreMed shares and quickly sold them as the price rose. Hooray—I earned $2,000. (By this time, I had stopped using mental quotation marks around the word *earned*.) It was easy, and I wanted more easy, so I bought some more shares.

CNBC caught the story on the news wires and talked it up. Bing—another $2,000. They teased a Joe Kernen segment on EntreMed after the close. The stock was still rising; angiostatin and endostatin now had a price per share of 25 and change. All the previous day's losses had been erased, and tomorrow the shorts—if there were any left— would be squeezed until their little piggy eyes popped out of their heads. *Give me another 500 shares to keep under my pillow, because tomorrow we cure cancer!* Ding. Ding. Ding. The market closed and I had gotten my shares and it was time to start wondering what the hell I was doing.

You see, in the quiet moments of the after-market, when only the ECNs are trading, a man has time to think. And this is what he thinks: he thinks that Bristol-Meyers, the pharmaceutical giant, was probably not caught completely by surprise when the National Cancer Institute announced its results. My ignorance of science is nearly complete, but I just couldn't imagine (and I tried, believe me) the NCI chemists or pharmacologists, or whatever the hell they were, racing out of their labs to the hallway telephone where, dialing 9 first for an outside line, connecting with a reporter at *The Boston Globe* and shouting, "Eureka!" For *The Boston Globe* to get the story, they probably had to read a press release or talk to an NCI official, who probably got the news from the scientists, who had probably finished measuring the last dwindling tumor on the last sick mouse some days or even weeks earlier.

Since the *Boston Globe* story reported that the NCI had used Folkman's lab at the Children's Hospital in Boston, it was a good guess that Folkman knew these results before

the *Globe* did. And if Folkman knew them, then Entre-
Med knew them. And if EntreMed knew them, Bristol-
Meyers probably learned about them in a conversation
that went something like: "Please, please, PLEASE don't
pull out of this now, just wait a few days, because the NCI
has duplicated the results, we swear!" And if Bristol-
Meyers, after calling a few of their friends at the NCI,
dropped angiostatin and endostatin anyway, then perhaps cancer was not quite as close to being cured as we all
thought when we were grabbing as many shares of Entre-
Med as our trading accounts could carry.

With these thoughts in mind, I had a clear goal. My goal
was to convince myself that I was just being paranoid,
that cancer was, in fact, nearly cured, and I was merely
suffering from a case of nerves. Failure to reach this goal
would cause at least one night of sleeplessness.

I looked forward to Joe Kernen's giving me some help
on CNBC, but I forgot that Joe Kernen has a degree in mo-
lecular biology. Kernen was calm, and signaled his scorn
for the 100 percent, one-day run-up in ENMD by arching
his eyebrow and giving a short description of how pro-
hibitively distant a functional medication was, even if the
NCI results held up.

"Joe Kernen hates everything," I told myself, trying to
overcome a slightly gaseous feeling in my brain. The
place to go for real support, I knew, was the message
boards on Silicon Investor, Raging Bull, The Motley Fool,
and Yahoo.

At first, I thought I was going to recover. "I feel sorry for anyone who is holding a short position overnight," wrote an EntreMed fan on Silicon Investor. "Remember last time it gapped to 80?"

Right on! I nearly shouted. Then I met Anthony.

ENMD<-------SELL/SHORT @ 26 1/2 (stock should trade around 7 to 8 based on 4 times cash)

Let's be realistic . . . they are years away from any thing that could possibly even come close to helping humans and are a decade away from any commercial use . . . We saw this before and we know what happened last time . . . The Bristol Myers news killed it and should not be discounted . . . There are those on this thread who claim to know more than the powers that be at Bristol Myers . . . ENMD is nothing but a pipe dream at this point in time and I have initiated coverage of this stock at current levels with an immediate Sell/SHORT

Who was this asshole? Didn't he know that I owned $13,000 worth of this breakthrough cancer cure, and that I needed to have that become at least $15,000, making my total profit $6,000 before taxes and almost completely wiping out my losses of the week before? Fortunately, other people dedicated to advances in oncology were quick to speak up. People who own stocks hate people who short them, and one of my new friends taunted Anthony with tomorrow's near-certain run-up:

The "true value" of the stock is irrelevant and impossible to gauge in any case--do you think it was worth 80 when the previous news came out? Now the studies have been replicated so it should be worth even more than it was before. It now had the NCI and the US government behind it--far more important the BMY.

Good luck with your short. Could see 50.

Suddenly, though, other shorts came out of the audience and joined Anthony in beating up on my stock. They seemed to know each other, and recited a long list of famous collapses that Anthony has supposedly called in public before they happened. "Yeah, sure," I sneered. People bragged like this all the time on Silicon Investor. It was easy to talk about making money after the fact. It was only the winners you saw, never the losers. And now I'd been at it long enough to know something about losers. Anthony's frequent, cruel posts bore a comforting resemblance to the hype that always popped up when something was happening with a volatile stock.

There was only one problem: what Anthony and his impolite pals were writing had a core of horrible common sense. A short named Pluvia, who apparently lived to rain on everybody's parade, wrote that "the REALLY BIG news came from BMY—and it went like this: 'We at BMY don't want to waste another cent on ENMD's volatile drug because we don't think it is commercially viable.' "

My defenders were reduced to counting on the irrationality of the average investor, arguing that the facts behind EntreMed were irrelevant now—only the publicity mattered. To me, this argument is infallible—except when it isn't. Like any mob, the hordes of quick traders who were pushing EntreMed around could change their mind overnight, and might now be in the process of doing just that.

Next thing I knew, Anthony had the bad taste to go read the documents EntreMed filed with the SEC, and to regale us with the awful news. He posted information about the price-to-cash ratios of other, similar biotech firms, arguing that ENMD ought to sell for 7 or 8 dollars. Pluvia moved on from facts to ridicule.

"Look," Pluvia wrote, "one of my crack SI cyber-snoop associates got this picture from the ENMD lab." People who followed the link found a Web animation of hundreds of squealing, singing, dancing rodents.

The damage went on late into the evening. It was simultaneously hilarious and humiliating. I knew I was sunk by ten o'clock, when one of the desperate cancer-fighters started comparing EntreMed to Yahoo and Amazon. "Of course they are overpriced," he whined, "but Internet stocks trade on potential, not earnings. Why can't a biotech stock do the same thing?"

You could practically hear Anthony giggling. "Internets trade where they do because they are generating revenues and have a 'potentially' unlimited market," he answered, pointing out that EntreMed had zero revenue and no products to date. "Sorry," he added, "but maybe you can find a 'cancercure.com' to buy." By midnight, my team was clearly beaten. The best anybody could do was to point out that the market would judge in the morning.

My goal of sleeping through the night was abandoned;

I now had a new goal. It was to get out of EntreMed as quickly as possible. I would try to sell in the premarket, when a few trades get made on the electronic trading networks. Taking a look at an ENMD Level II window at the first blush of premarket trading, it was clear I had the right approach. There were no buyers. ENMD was definitely going to gap down. It was early enough that selling hadn't hit in force quite yet, so I watched ENMD's quiet screen for a moment, and when nobody else was selling, I put out an ask at 24⅞. This was almost a dollar beneath where I'd bought, but it was on the high end of the few morning sells that had already executed. After thirty painful seconds, a miracle occurred. I found a buyer. Within five minutes ENMD's premarket trading had dropped to 23; later it went as low as 20. Although the official price at the open was 23⁹⁄₁₆, this is misleading, because that was the high for the day, and the price fell fast. When I posted my exit price, the traders in Ken's room who'd held EntreMed overnight—and there were many—could scarcely believe I'd managed to find someone to pay so dear a price for my shares. I didn't care whether they believed me or not. I was just happy to hold on to my thousands of dollars of profit. Had I hesitated for five minutes, I'd have lost it all and then some.

Of course I was very curious about Anthony.

"The public is there for one reason and one reason only," said Anthony when I got him on the phone. "They are there to absorb the risk. Brokers, broker-dealers, professional traders, they are not interested in any kind of risk whatsoever. They're interested in covered profits and arbitrage. They sell you the stock up here, they know they'll get it back down here."

Anthony's last name is Elgindy, and his first name, officially, is Amr. He is from Cairo, and he used to be a broker-dealer himself before NASD regulations and fines that he considers unreasonable forced him out of business. Now he plays the market as a retail customer, but with the tools and attitude of the professional. Since he doesn't have the honor of his fellow broker-dealers to defend, and is no longer regulated by the Association, he is free to speak harshly of them. Like the SOES pioneers, Elgindy is an outsider looking in, and he fervently believes that Nasdaq market makers regularly manipulate stock prices to get the better of their customers.

Anthony's theory is that when stocks run up big, the brokers sell short on every jump and cover on every pullback. Since brokers don't have to worry about margin calls from their broker, they can short with impunity. They can start shorting more as the buying pauses, watch the stock tick down, and start covering as it drops. The drop will shake out some overenthusiastic buyers who bought at the top, and these new sellers provide the shares that the brokers are buying.

"Today," said Anthony, "one major broker put out a buy recommendation on six stocks. You know they were shorting all of these stocks, and I know that tomorrow eToys, which was one of them, will be down two bucks. I know that for a fact. I don't even have to worry about it. I don't have to write it down. I don't have to put up any money. I don't have to bet. I don't have to pray. I just know it will happen because they were shorting into the rise. They are on the other side of your trade. The person who bought eToys this morning at forty-eight, his broker sold it to him and did it happily with a smile, and he probably thanked him for it after he bought it."

Naturally, I checked the stock the next day. EToys, which had made a quick two-week run from 30 to reach 48 the day of our interview, hit 48 once again the next day and then dropped 8 gut-wrenching points back to 40. I presume Anthony made a lot of money.

Anthony's view of the market is uniformly black. He believes that corporate accounting is bogus, that press releases are untrue, and that Wall Street is "the most manipulated scam and corrupt marketplace on earth right now." The more disorderly the markets, the easier it is for the professionals to take advantage of the amateurs. Entre-Med had its high for the day at the open, though it showed much lower prices in pre-open trading. This means that somebody—probably a market maker—sold ENMD to somebody else—probably a retail customer whose order was waiting in line from the night before—at 23$\frac{9}{16}$. Anthony pictures the mainstream Nasdaq market as an evil partnership between the new online brokerages and the old-line trading houses with whom they are supposed to be competing. The online brokerages bring new herds of sheep into the game and collect the admission fees, while the market makers do the shearing.

"Right now," Anthony continued, "people just get wild

hairs up their ass and all of a sudden a whole sector will move and there is no rhyme or reason to it. A perfect example is online banking. Net banks are at twenty or thirty bucks and then they shoot up to two hundred because everybody is talking about how people will do more banking online, and over a four-month period they drop back down to twenty bucks. The more volatile the market, the more risk associated with it, and undoubtedly the more losers. You have the public versus the professional and the public is going to lose in the end. All the flaws you see today will finally be addressed at some point but not until the public has lost billions."

Anthony once tried to work for a major market maker, Bear Stearns, but found the atmosphere uncongenial. His stint with the brokerage lasted less than three months. Relations between Anthony and his employer were so strained that Anthony began going to work with a tape recorder secreted on his person, seeking evidence to use in case of a lawsuit. (Anthony did sue his ex-employer, but his tape recordings were ruled inadmissible and he lost the suit.) While I'd noticed that many of the day-trading gurus had a whiff of outlawry about them, Anthony's was even stronger than usual. He'd appeared on national television, telling ABC's *20/20* that the Nasdaq market was full of organized criminals running up stocks and defrauding the public. He worked at home with loaded guns nearby, he told me, to defend himself against death threats. His conflicts with the administrators of Nasdaq made it unlikely he would trade professionally again. Like a cashiered naval officer who turns privateer,

Anthony had converted his battles in the brokerage business into a righteous campaign against illegitimate authority.

Rightly timed, such a move can be lucrative. Like Ken Wolff and Doug Fairclough and Jeffrey Citron and Joshua Levine and the Townsends, and Bear Stearns, and Charles Schwab, and CNBC, Anthony has discovered that the best business in the bull market is helping other people get into it. A subscription to Anthony's private Web site, which includes access to all of his recommendations, costs $600 a month. This is top dollar—well over twice the price of Ken Wolff's mtrader. Plus, many of Anthony's subscribers recently came up with several thousand dollars to watch Anthony trade in person. On a Friday morning, very early, I went to the ballroom of a San Diego hotel to watch the first day of the trading seminar Anthony organized for his devoted followers.

Anthony rushed the podium amidst a flurry of spotlights and a decibel-crunching sampled medley of pro-sports jingo. "Y'all ready for this?" asked a thunderous prerecorded voice. "Are you ready to rumble?!" But things quieted down quickly and Anthony settled into his silent business. The stage was flanked by two large screens, which showed the Level II order flow. Anthony, being a professional, doesn't bother with Real Tick from Townsend Analytics. He uses the industry standard: Bloomberg. The students were both impressed and bothered by this. They don't use Bloomberg terminals. Does this make them losers?

After a morning of watching the markets and lecturing

on the evils of the market makers, Anthony used the last half hour of the trading day to put on an amazing performance combining stand-up comedy with real-time moneymaking—complete with a guest appearance by Verne Troyer, the midget star from the recently released *The Spy Who Shagged Me.* While trading quips with Mini-Me, Anthony, who is a bit of a bully, presented a made-to-order comical victim to the audience. The victim was a company called Stamps.com.

Stamps.com was seeking approval from the United States Postal Service to sell postage over the Internet. They went public on June 25, 1999, at 11 and immediately jumped to 22¾. A few days later, the stock ran up again—pushed to above 30 by a meaningless public relations announcement of a marketing partnership with another frothy darling of day traders, MySoftware Company.* At 30, Stamps.com, an untried company that had yet to sell a single stamp online, had a valuation of more than a billion dollars. It was EntreMed all over again.

A press conference was scheduled for the following Monday morning, at which the Postal Service was expected to announce that commercial Internet companies like Stamps.com would be granted permission to sell postage online. This would not be an exclusive license for

---

* Later, when I looked up the press release touting the partnership, I discovered that MySoftware.com's claim to fame was not its products but its stock price. The company announced itself as "the ninth-best performer on all U.S. capital markets in 1998."

Stamps.com, but it was a key step in the company's business plan; or rather, it was a key step in the company's plan to someday have a business. To Anthony, it was an ideal opportunity to make money. "This has got some of the best ingredients in the world for a trade," he told his audience, speaking rapidly as he watched the price rise on his Bloomberg screens. "You've got a magic day, you've got a magic number, we've got *magic*. We've got a definite target. We have a climax point, what everybody is shooting for."

Because Stamps.com was still in its start-up phase and had no customers, no sales, no revenue, and therefore no profits, the owners of the company's stock needed other benchmarks by which to judge its success. In this context, the expected announcement by the Postal Service counted as brilliant news. "Everybody is looking for some specific thing to happen," Anthony continued, "and when it happens, the world will be great; the sun will shine; Saturn, Jupiter, and the moon will all be aligned properly; cancer will be cured; and all wars will stop. And when it happens, they all do the same thing." He paused to set up the punch line. "They all run for the exits."

We had seen STMP open that morning at 26¾. As the minutes of the session ticked by, the price soared. Five minutes before the close, Anthony sold short 2000 shares at 36. He was watching the screens. "Take a look now," he grinned. "You'll see, on the bid you have *only* ECNs." This made him happy. "You have no market makers. All just day traders. Two hundred shares. Three hundred shares. Two hundred shares. They do not represent the Mensa society." Every once in a while a huge bid for 10,000 shares would appear on the screen, then quickly evaporate. Since no trades of ten thousand shares were showing as prints, Anthony surmised that what we were seeing was wise-guy day traders flashing offers they never intended to keep, in order to create the illusion that there was "buying interest." With his broker on the phone, Anthony announced his intention to sell to one of these clowns (sell short, of course) if he had a chance. Besides delighting the crowd, such a move would have two additional benefits: it would allow him to swing a very large line short on STMP, which he was looking to do, while also leaving some fidgety day trader with 10,000 more shares that he would doubtless seek to unload in a panicky fashion at the first sign of weakness, adding to the massive "selling interest," also known as panic. Sadly, the big bids flashed too quickly to grab, and Anthony ended the day—and his stage routine—short a mere 2000 shares.

Anthony suspected that there might be more buying after the weekend, and he was looking forward to selling more if the stock went up. But now the market was closed, and he'd done all he could. "Okay, that's all we're going to get," he sighed. "I'm short two thousand Stamps.com. It was really simple to know that people were going to want to get long right before the market closes in anticipation of the big news come Monday morning, the big news which will undoubtedly disappoint. Could it go up a couple of points more? Sure, but that's just a good opportunity to continue building your position."

By Monday, the longs and the shorts were going at each other on the message boards with the rhetorical subtlety of World Wrestling Federation wannabes screaming their lungs out in the parking lot of a tavern in Fresno. "MAN I hope you got your Tissue ready, how much did you short??? God man . . . burn city," wrote one long on Silicon Investor, where Anthony and his friends were unleashing their usual schoolyard taunts. When the market opened, the stock quickly ran up past 40, and Elgindy called another short on the stock at 42. By the end of the day, it was the shorts who were crowing. "Meltdown!" screamed one, when the stock dropped below 34. "I have my tissue ready," gloated another, answering the earlier post. "I use it to wipe turds like STMP off the bottom of my shoe."

A good number of Elgindy's students had whipped out their cell phones and sold STMP along with their teacher. Others made their trades on Monday morning when the stock gapped up. They had beaten the game by anticipating the reaction of their day-trading competitors. Slower traders, and ones not attuned to the short-selling game, had perhaps wandered home from a job on Friday night and found STMP on the list of the day's gainers, and blithely bought in anticipation of the news. As a group, they had lost millions.*

Perhaps it was only fair that the people beaten by Anthony and the other short-sellers were mostly day traders

---

* In the following months, Stamps.com would continue its fun fluctuations, peaking at 98 before dropping back below 40.

and foolhardy amateurs. Such are the risks of the pari-mutel. It is impossible to exaggerate the hatred between the longs and the shorts when a speculative battle gets hot. For a bit of fun, I called up TokyoJoe and asked him what he thought of Anthony. "I don't consider him a human being," he answered. He then turned anthropologist. "Have you noticed that all shorts have the same physical characteristics?" he asked. "They all have mean eyes, a crooked mouth line, and their shoulders are never even. This is because they look at the world in a twisted way."

I didn't mind instigating a fight between the opposing generals in the war between the longs and the shorts because they both were clearly enjoying the engagement. The sharp blasts of invective benefited them both by attracting onlookers, pumping up the crowd, and extracting a great nourishing gush of dumb money.

CHAPTER EIGHT

THE SLEEP
OF REASON

2:00 A.M. PST

Night, for me, is merely pre-morning. The action on the message boards is slowing down by two A.M. I pick up my Chinese medicine balls and roll and jangle them in my hand; this is supposed to ease the pain. I chew my last Nicorette. Being a winner means thinking like a winner, I tell myself, attempting a couple of end-of-day visualization techniques. I am asking a bank teller if she can cash a check for ten thousand dollars. I am sending a jeroboam of something French away from my table, saying, "No, bigger." I am selling fistfuls of the latest Internet issue short into massive buying, with no worry about a margin call. It isn't working. Sleep is out of the question.

I am lying here thinking about my days of caressing Oracle's gentle curves. The relationship did not end well. My favorite position stock had been hanging around in a tight range for weeks. It had support at 37, there was resistance at 40, and it zigzagged back and forth between these two numbers a few times every day. Profit was assured. I could build up a nice cushion of cash in anticipation of a minor loss and keep a tight stop if the stock dropped unexpectedly. After a week, I had a nice safety net. I'd buy at around 38½ on the way up and sell at 39½ before it headed back down.

Then one day Oracle caught me off guard with weaker highs and lower lows. During a slight afternoon rally I picked it up at 35½ and sold it at 36, then picked it up at 36$\frac{9}{16}$ and sold it at 36$\frac{11}{16}$, and so on. I was doing alright, until something happened that I hadn't exactly planned for. The trading day ended. And so did Oracle's predictable cycling. After the bell, Oracle would announce its earnings, and the war between the bulls and the bears, so evenly matched for so long, would be decided one way or the other. On a whim, I stayed long at 36⅞.

Why, after EntreMed, did this happen again? I paused for introspection. Thinking, thinking . . . there! I had it. The reason I was long overnight is that I *believed* in Oracle. I knew the Net was exploding, I knew Oracle was providing lots of database software, I knew they were going to succeed. I had faith that over the long term this company was a great investment.

Perhaps I needed to see a psychologist. "Doctor, please give me something to take my mind off reality."

Predictably, Oracle beat earnings estimates. But only by a penny. And that was only with the benefit of a one-time sale of stock in a subsidiary. This was a disaster. Since the big customers who keep large inventories of stocks—mutual funds and pension plans and the like—are staffed by people who understand accounting, they know that a corporation will pull every trick in the book to bring their earnings in above expectations. ("Expectations" are set by the company in meetings with analysts—a system like the now discredited self-directed grading schemes you may have experienced if you went to school in America in the seventies.) When a company misses expectations, or barely beats them with the assistance of accounting legerdemain, it's clear they are suffering. The institutional investors will disappear for a while, figuring that if they want more Oracle it will be easy to get some cheaper, later. The day traders will disappear because there isn't any momentum. In the after-hours session, there were no buyers for Oracle. The asks just got lower and lower: 35, 34, 33. As low as 32. *It must be an overreaction,* I thought.

I'm not selling at these levels, it'll be fine in the morning, I tried to persuade myself. And then I started to whimper, and recited my own special prayer for moments like these, which in the name of full disclosure, I will confess to here. It goes: "Baby J. Christ in a buckskin yurt, please get me out before I get hurt."

At five the next morning, I stared out my windows onto banks of fog that looked dirty under the streetlights. What I was seeing on my screen was mass murder, and I was part of the mass. Those rock-bottom ORCL prints at 33 and 32 I saw after close weren't the rock bottom, after all.

ORCL was fading below 30. That was 6⅞ or so less than I paid for it a minute before the close. A word came back to me, a word that day traders use to describe themselves when all the rules are broken and everything that can go wrong does. The word is *investor.*

Was I going to become an Oracle investor? Or was I going to eat another big chunk of last year's eBay profits for breakfast? Going broke once or twice, I've been told, is the price of admission. But, you know, I really didn't want to go broke. I didn't think I could handle going broke. EBay was the luckiest financial windfall I had ever had in my life—maybe the luckiest I ever would have. I wanted more lucky windfalls. If I wanted to pay a six-figure tuition to learn how to do something that required a humiliating apprenticeship and an iron constitution, I would have tried to become a doctor, or learned to play polo.

I came to day trading looking for a way out of the chaos of blind betting, of surprise swings that could make or break me. The rules I found seemed simple: look for the easy win, don't take unnecessary risks, nobody ever went broke taking profits. But when the crucial moment comes—and it comes every day—the sheer unknowability of the future gets in the way. Every story of blown stops and hair-raising rides down a steep decline mentions the sensation I was feeling as I watched thousands of dollars disappear by the second into the sinking pit of the Oracle sell orders. I was the earthquake victim who forgets to run out from beneath a wall when it falls. I was the big-eyed doe standing still on the highway as the headlights bear down. Every option was terrible. It was wrong to do nothing, but nothing was all I could do.

I'd long delighted in the misfortune of strangers. Last fall, when the incautious short-sellers of eBay were getting mown down like grass on a sunny fairway, I would read their posts on the Yahoo boards and savor their plight. One day, I came across this note:

> I was short Ebay at 52, 4000 shares by: ZEEBA__1 2724 of 68824
>
> My broker just covered my 4000, with negative of 22,000. I can not face my family tonight, I thing I am going to kill my self lost 400,000 everything I had make last fifteen years in my retail business.

A suicide note? Far-fetched, but entertaining. He was probably a long who wanted to discourage anybody from selling. Before the people on the board could decide, another unfortunate correspondent popped up.

> I ran out of money by: mandbilli 2791 of 68824
>
> Hope will not die before I run out of sleeping pills, lost last penny today, actually I am in debt right now. Shorted at 49 3/4, my wife goes to college and I pay her tuition, nothing left, nothing left. But there is a god who will take care of these people who stole my money and others by manipulating this stock. It is true that I have limited experience, but I followed briefing.com advice that ebay was way overvalued at 50. I am sorry to bore

you with my situation, but may be it is the only way to avoid killing my self.

As I sat there marveling, a good Samaritan tried some long-distance therapy. "It's only money," she posted. I contemplated this phrase for a moment, trying to understand its meaning. Moments later the tide shifted, and the true spirit of Yahoo came into play. Words of encouragement started filling the eBay discussion screens:

hope you by: biker64 (44/M/tacoma, wa) 2905 of 68824

BK you get what you deserve, when you short a stock you are hurting all longs and you don't care so take your pills and go to sleep. Just don't come back to short again and hurt another long. HAHA HAHA HAHA

Others joined in. Like a crowd gathered underneath a stockbroker on a ledge, they shouted for Zeeba and Mandbilli to jump and be quick about it. "Hurry up," they cried. "Do it!" I understood the impulse. Who were these goofballs, anyway, who intruded with their meddling short-selling and constant criticism? They deserved nothing better than a fistful of sleeping pills and a one-person slumber party in a bathroom stall. Day trading is not a win-win business. When you win, somebody else loses.

Make that, a lot of people lose. During the summer of 1999, a lot of bad news appeared. Academic students of market timing, using carefully constructed studies, demonstrated that while the financial results of perfect timing were seductive, they were virtually unreachable. A widely publicized study of a group of All-Tech traders showed that the winners were likely to be people who made a lot of money on a single good trade and managed not to lose it all on the rest of their (bad) trades.

A lot of money on a single good trade. I may have made most of my big money on a handful of trades instead of just one, but it still sounded terribly familiar. In *Reminiscences of a Stock Operator,* which is based on the career of Jesse Livermore, Edwin Lefevre describes with ruthless candor the mentality of the failing amateur: "Suckers differ among themselves according to the degree of experience. The tyro knows nothing, and everybody, including himself, knows it. But the next, or second grade thinks he knows a great deal and makes others feel that way too . . . It is this semi-sucker rather than the 100 percent article who is the real all-year-round support of the commission houses."

And yet, hadn't I discovered, beneath the hype and the obvious cons, a few people who were actually very good at knowing what the market was going to do? Sure, a lot of people lose. So what? A lot of restaurants fail. A lot of college stars don't make the NBA. Who says I'm one of the losers?

Lying awake in bed, waiting for the alarm to go off and give me permission to stop trying to sleep, I mentally review my trading results from the last twenty-four hours. In the morning I almost slipped on a banana peel; I wanted to buy more Liquid Audio when it was running, and I stopped myself just before it slid back. Though I didn't make money, I saved myself from an ugly loss, which is almost as good. At midday I almost got a ride on one of the stupid Internet plays that made me so much money in the past, but I didn't pull the trigger in time. No money lost, but I missed three quick points on the way up, and it pretty much feels like a loss. But I can congratulate myself that, thanks partly to Doug, I didn't make any fatal mistakes at the close. All in all, the day was a wash. One trade up, if I'd done it, one down, if I'd done it; and I avoided going over the cliff.

I'm trying to tell myself this isn't as futile as it sounds. The fact is, it's been very hard to actually make a trade lately. I keep watching and waiting for that amazing "you can't lose" feeling to come back, but instead, my sense of impending doom only gets stronger.

Robin Dayne, whom I met through Ken Wolff, is a trading coach who specializes in people who have lost confidence. Most of them are worse off than me, because when they start going downhill they deal with it by making more and more trades, hoping a win will get them back in the groove. When I called her to find out what kind of help she offered, Dayne let me know that business had been increasing since Mark Barton started shooting people.

"This doesn't seem like the time when there would be a lot of people asking how to become a day trader," I opined.

But I was wrong, according to Dayne. "A lot of people never knew day trading existed. They never knew the potential in it. When they find out, they say, 'How the heck do I do that?' "

I found this amazing. " 'How the heck do I lose a hundred and fifty thousand dollars a month?' "

"Yes," she said. "It has stirred it up."

Dayne told me that she was recently working at a trading firm in New York as a trainer, and one day she was interrupted by an employee who came running into the room. He requested her assistance.

"What's the matter?" Dayne asked the employee.

"A guy's ready to jump out the window."

"Where is he?" she inquired.

"We left him there," answered the employee.

This didn't seem like the right thing to do, so Dayne went quickly over to the man who was thinking about killing himself and began to talk with him about his family. After a few minutes, he changed his mind. But Dayne reports that three people attempted suicide in the two years she worked at the firm, and one succeeded.

Dayne nonetheless believes that trading is a great career if you can manage your emotions. Emotional management is her specialty, so if that part is bothering you she can help. Her techniques include a proprietary cognitive exercise she calls "the scramble." I think I may need to use it someday, but she doesn't want to give me any details because it is too valuable. She promised to write a book eventually and explain the whole thing.

I expressed some skepticism about day trading as a career. Perhaps it was my troubled state of mind, but I had started to think of day trading less as an occupation, and more as a neurosis, or worse.

"I wonder if some people go into day trading for the same reason that they might turn to gambling or alcohol or some other form of self-destruction," I said to Dayne, unable to resist provoking her a little.

"It's not an addiction," said Dayne, gratifyingly annoyed. "It is a business and people work very hard in it. There's no other business, positively nothing on earth that you can spend one year of training and make this amount of cash. There's nothing! Name one thing. There's nothing!"

"Um, what amount of cash are you thinking of?" I asked.

"Well, a good consistent trader makes an average of a thousand dollars per day. That's a nice living. You know you don't have to go for the big bucks. You don't have to make a million dollars a year. You can live very nicely on a thousand a day, or even five hundred a day. What jobs do you know that you can make five hundred a day and maybe work two hours. Certainly not as a magazine writer!"

"No," I admitted. "Nope." Then again, I thought to myself, I've never actually *lost* money on a writing assignment.

The question occurred to me, and not for the first time, that if some people were making a thousand dollars per day on short-term trades, where was the money coming from?

"Can everybody make money simultaneously?" I asked, trying to see if I lived on the same mathematical planet as Dayne did.

"Yes," Dayne said firmly. "Every day there is a new IPO."

A thousand dollars a day. To clear a thousand dollars a day, after brokerage commissions, capital gains taxes, spreads, and fees for equipment, Internet connectivity, and information services, you have to have about two thousand a day in gross trading profits. It sounds so easy. The problem comes when your first trade ticks down and you cut your losses and get out only $150 behind. A small victory, but now you have to clear $2,150 that day—if this is an average day. One day-trading report compared betting on incremental moves of the ticker to betting on a coin toss, except that it is possible for the coin to land on its side. Even a flat trade costs money.

And yet I knew it was not a scam. What about Ken? What about Doug? What about Anthony? I had looked closely enough to know that they weren't lying about their trading methods. Hell, I'd just read an article in *The Washington Post* about Lawrence Black, a twenty-seven-year-old amateur who made more than a million dollars in the first three months of 1999 alone. All of these phenomenal winners could clearly follow the tape. They could call good trades. Was I a man or a mouse?

In the long line for lunch at Anthony's seminar, I had met two women who, when we got talking, admitted with embarrassed smiles that they hadn't yet got the hang of shorting stocks. One of them was wearing a name tag that said "soccermom." The other was heavyset and dark-haired, and I didn't catch her name because it was hidden behind her arm; she held her hand modestly near her face while she talked. The dark-haired woman was a little ashamed by her unconventional approach to investing. She had doubled her money speculating in penny stocks traded on the Vancouver exchange, capital of fraudulent stock schemes and unscrupulous touts. She was looking for a better way. After her stint on the Vancouver exchange, she had turned to Anthony.

Another attendee, with the bitter wisdom of a veteran campaigner, told me that brokers are called brokers "because they make you broke." He started trading on his own eighteen months ago, after losing much of his savings following his broker's advice. He was looking for a better savior.

A fourth person I talked to told a devastating tale of sitting at a recital at his daughter's school, knowing that he couldn't meet his broker's margin call, and saying to himself, as he calculated his losses, "There goes the house, and there goes the car, and there goes the college fund, and there. . . ." He called it one of the most horrible experiences of his life.

These are the heroes of the long boom, relative innocents who believe it is perfectly reasonable to try to double their money monthly in the stock market, if only somebody will let them in on the secret.

I liked meeting all these people, but it was clear as day that—at least by today's capitalist calculus—they were natural losers. Like Houtkin and some of the other SOES pioneers, they are outsiders who want in, but they are unseasoned by sharp competition in the world of the small-time hustle. And while Doug and Anthony and Ken and TokyoJoe and Reverend Shark all knew how to trade and make money, they had all built thriving businesses of a different nature, charging admission fees to these rank amateurs.

Was it wrong of them? Hard to say. Anthony's picks are uncanny; Ken's advice indisputable; Doug's Web site actually lovable in its innocent, sincere opacity. But the gulf between the winners and losers is evident. There's Ken, the elk hunter, and then there's Ken's brother, who stands in awe and forgets to shoot. There's Anthony with his deadly short picks, and there are the hapless subscribers who can't quite catch the best moment, and then jump on, and then can't manage to get out in time. And as for Doug, he's a trading loner who's already gone broke twice; he has built a tool that helps him with his arcane figurations but that is unlikely to transform the odds even for the people who can figure out how to use it.

I made money as a day trader—but in a knock-out sense only if you include the string of lucky strikes I had on E*Trade, which hardly count as true day trades. I've had moments of almost criminal profit-making—episodes where taking money out of the market was as effortless as dipping my head into a cool stream for a sip of water.

These have been countered by equally swift losses, where it seemed like my head was wedged tight between two rocks beneath that same stream.

Indeed, looking back over my account history I find many instances of very rough trade. Most of the time, I look at the Nasdaq symbols on my execution statements and can't even remember the name of the company, much less why I was trading it. MSTG, OPTN, ONEM, ICOS, TWLB: these are meaningless things to me, though I let tens of thousands of dollars ride on them without a minute's hesitation. Did I make money on them? Sometimes. But usually not enough, I'm forced to admit in my more sober moments, to justify the risks. And looking back at the riskier maneuvers I've been party to, it looks like summertime livin' on boob beach. Why not let's use this syringe I found as a back-scratcher? Why not let's do some naked wrasslin' with those jellyfish? Why not let's trade an IPO?

Let's take a look at my IPO trading. There's me jumping in and out of Autoweb (AWEB on the Nasdaq) a half-dozen times or so on its first day out. I am taking 500-share lots. I make $31 on my first trade; $781 on my second trade; $156 on the third; $44 on my fourth; $13 on my fifth; and I somehow decide to take 300 shares home overnight. One day later and seven points and change higher, I've made another $2,100, which only reinforces the bad habit. Each of those gains could just have easily been losses. Three days later, Autoweb's largest competitor starts trading. I'm in for 300 shares at $56^{11}/_{16}$. By the time I manage to get a sell order through—and trust me,

I'm trying every point down—the price is at 50¾. That's $1,781.25 in losses, plus $45.90 in commissions plus fifty-one cents SEC fee, for a grand total instaloss of $1,827.66. Taken together, these two episodes gave me three days of all-night anxiety for a profit of roughly a grand. Not a bad daily take. But how much was the misery worth? How much was the lost hair worth? How much for the pain in the pit of my stomach? Using Robin Dayne's $500-per-day standard, I was already $500 behind, *before taxes.*

And that's also before the fantasy arithmetic sets in, the speculative economics that had me wondering six months ago whether I could make twice as much if I spent twice the time playing the markets. Whether I could make ten times as much if I spent less time in each stock and caught only the wild swings. At the end of a harsh trading day, the mental calculator comes out and does its damage. What if I had just held on to EBAY? If I hadn't sold it at 140 and had instead held it right to 700, I'd have become a millionaire in a single trade. If I'd held those first couple hundred Microsoft shares I'd bought on E*Trade to try out my account, I'd have done at least as well as I'd done with all those dozens of daily trades. If I'd only stayed in the mutual funds whose performance had disgusted me enough to motivate me into stocks in the first place, I'd have . . . well, I'd have lost another $10,000 and been really, really resentful of my neighbors.

In this way, hindsight first goes out of focus, then becomes muddled entirely. Clearly, my entrance into the markets was well timed—though I can hardly take credit for that. Some of my investment decisions were probably even a little bit smart. But becoming an active day trader was, for me, an exercise in diminishing returns. Was there ever a perfect balance struck, a one-drink-per-hour happy medium that would allow me to enjoy the party without totaling my car? Something that didn't have me up at market open and still awake at midnight, contemplating certain doom the next morning? Or was the insanity less about market strategy than about my vivid fantasies of other people's accelerating profit; that auriferous horizon that invites you to spend not only your daytime hours, and not only your nighttime hours, but also your real reserves of nonhypothetical funds in an attempt to reach the cash-green oasis of winners?

These doubts had been building for months, and I'd had many chances to solicit a second opinion. The morning after my harrowing overnight Oracle hold, I sent a message to Ken. "Don't know how I've managed to get myself in this position, but stupidly, I'm holding ORCL. Not a small position, either. Any opinion on whether it'll bounce?" Ken promised to follow it that morning. Which he did. It wasn't just for my benefit—apparently, I was not the only fool in his crowd. Ken did a pretty good job spotting strength in ORCL, wherever he could find it, but it was no use. ORCL was weak and getting weaker. It went below 30 and when it came back briefly, I started selling. When I finally got out completely, ORCL was trading in the mid-29s. For once, I tried not to do the math. Thankfully, my mouse pad, so helpful in calculating the profits and losses on sixteenths, doesn't extend into losses of multiple points on 1400 shares. But even if I didn't know the dollar amount, I knew it was bad. This was the wreck you slow down to watch, only to be plunged into the horror of recognizing the demolished car as your own. When you come to in the ambulance, you vow to share your story with schoolchildren and Bible study groups and to make a lifetime career out of giving people the creeps.

After I took my beating on Oracle, I sent another message to Ken, telling him that I sold my shares and accepted my losses. He told me that taking the hit and moving on shows that I'm a good trader. He also told me never to front-run earnings, with which I concur from the deepest crannies of my soul. This is the kind of loss that makes you wonder how many different ways there are of saying, "Never again," and whether you could ever live long enough to say them all. I won't front-run earnings ever again. With this recollection fresh in my mind, I don't think I'm going to be back-running earnings, side-running news, drug-running biotechs, or doing much running at all today. I hear the sound of a truck rumbling down the alley next to my loft. It must be nearly morning. I have made it through another night. I reach for the Nicorette, but as I grope at the nightstand I knock my clock off the table. "Shit," I mutter, "now I'm going to miss the open." And then, for the first time in what seems like weeks, I sleep.*

---

*In the first days of January 2000, some ten months after I'd sold out my position in the mid-29s, ORCL shares were trading for more than 120 per share.

EPILOGUE

I missed a number of market opens after that morning. By the time I got out of bed the construction crews had been shouting at each other for hours, and when they woke me up I reacted not with my usual string of anally fixated middle-school curses but with a slow blink of relief. I was almost comfortable. The more market openings I missed, the more at ease I felt. I was like a person watching dreamily from the dock as a millionaire's yacht slipped form its berth into the blue-gray edge of a storm. I might not be rich, but at least I wasn't on that boat.

Boat . . . millionaire . . . not rich . . . hey, what time was it? Nearly noon. And what had I done with myself during the past weeks? Nearly nothing. Oh, sure, I'd made it into work semiregularly and schemed to liberate my Web site from the clutches of its absentee landlords, but during this pleasant pause in my day-trading career I'd made no progress toward the winner's circle, which all the while had been welcoming newcomers—not including me—at a busy pace. While I was napping, Foundry Networks went public and traded at more than 500 percent over the offering price on its first day. Foundry Networks was down in Sunnyvale. I wondered if I knew somebody there.

What went wrong? Had I really reconciled myself to a life of quiet . . . of quiet . . . of quiet something or other? I reached for my *Bartlett's*. "The mass of men lead lives of quiet desperation," said H. Thoreau, and from my quick perusal of his extracts I guessed he was a failed trader, because he seemed somewhat depressed about money.

I was not ready, not yet, to consign myself to poverty and virtue. I was not a failed trader. Beginning with $50,000, I had banged my way up to $150,000 in just a few months. Even after a series of unfortunate executions and slightly delusional short-term predictions I still found myself up more than 100 percent on the year. I had doubled my stake, and then some. I was a long way from my million dollars, but before I threw in the towel and declared myself a philosopher I needed to know what, if anything, separated me from the trading demigods whose names, by the summer of 1999, had begun to circulate in the press.

The trader whose story fascinated me most was Lawrence Black. He traded from a personal computer in his mother's basement and claimed to have regular days of $100,000 in trading profits. Black confidently predicted he would soon have his first million-dollar day. My friends took sadistic delight in clipping stories about traders who were more successful than me; I got two separate envelopes in the mail containing a *Washington Post* story calling Black "a master of the new universe" and "the biggest trader the world has never heard of." Black was twenty-seven years old. If I met him, would I see my future? Or would I see something else, some hint of superior knowledge or self-control that explained his fabulous wealth?

I didn't feel I could call Lawrence and ask him to submit to an examination by experts. How could I set up the right conditions for a comparison between him and me?

Luck intervened. Lawrence Black was scheduled to appear at the first international exposition of day traders and day-trading firms, to be held in Ontario in September. Nearly every other major player in the day-trading world would be joining him there. Black was announced as the guest of honor at a special conference event: a panel of six independent traders who had each made—or so it was claimed—a million dollars in trading profits in the past year.

Ontario, California, is east of Los Angeles, not far from Rancho Cucamonga. It is Mike Davis country, where your plane drops precipitously into an all-concealing smog, and where the empty airport and free-at-a-moment's-notice convention center suggest unimaginative regional corruption. As I sat at a plastic table waiting for the first workshops, I overheard two men talking nearby. Since I am an experienced eavesdropper, I knew not to turn and look at them.

"If I pay attention and keep my concentration I can make money," said one. "But my mind wanders and I think about other things—and I lose."

I found this difficult to comprehend. When I was trading my life savings, I got cramps in my hand from gripping the mouse.

The trader then began talking about a recent market-rattling statement by a Microsoft executive that the company's stock was overvalued. "I was in the next room playing my sax when the news came out," he said. "When I came back the market had lost a hundred points. I looked at it and thought, we're bottoming. And then, *whoosh,* the market lost another hundred points. How can you know something like that is going to happen?"

His friend clucked sympathetically. He knew the next, bitter confession as well as I did, and he obligingly supplied it: "The problem is, things like that *always* happen!"

If these were the kind of people I was trading against, it was no wonder I doubled my money. I turned slightly for a surreptitious glance. Two elderly white men were sitting there, quietly now, each musing on his own losses.

Across the table from me, eating breakfast from a Styrofoam container, was a young Asian man in a blue blazer who didn't seem the type to blow scales while the tech stocks were crashing. I asked if he had been trading long.

"Two years," he answered. His name was Henry and he was trading with savings from his day job at a big brokerage firm plus some money he had borrowed from his parents. He was twenty-six, and had moved to the United States from China when he was seven. His goal was to start his own business, but he needed capital. He intended to keep trading until he got married, after which he expected his wife to force him to stop.

Henry's trading account had sometimes held as much as $150,000. His "style," if you want to call it that, was frighteningly similar to mine: he bought popular technology stocks and held on while they ran. He was particularly attracted to the stocks of companies headquartered in California. "If I see the company is from California, then I'm interested in buying it," he said. His total earnings, over his two years of trading, came to about $50,000. It would be more, he explained, but in July he lost $85,000 in two weeks. He had been pondering this experience lately and feeling very bad. I told Henry I was trying to get to the bottom of my obsession with day trading and that I might even write a book about it. "If you are going to write a book," he said, "tell people not to lose too much money. It's terrible."

I met quite a few people like Henry at the Expo: semi-experienced traders who weren't quite satisfied with their approach. Their ages ranged widely, but they shared a self-conscious rejection of naïveté. They knew, and wanted to make sure I knew, that it was possible to lose money. Many were small net winners from their experiments in the market, and they were eager to move up into a bigger league.

The conference, organized in just a few months by a couple of Southern California traders, was a stupendous success. More than two thousand traders showed up. The exhibit floor was full of very young people voicing boasts about their role in the new economic revolution. The next Expo, planned for a few months later, would not be in a smog-choked valley of the Inland Empire but at the Jacob Javits Convention Center in Manhattan, within easy reach of the networks and CNBC.

On the exhibit floor, booths from scores of companies pitched products for beating the market. Omar Amanat from Tradescape was there, showing off his Web-based trading platform and touting his bargain-basement fees. Ken Wolff was there, explaining that slow and steady wins the race. Harvey Houtkin was there, bragging about the money he'd taken out of SOES and loudly proclaiming his refusal to "go mainstream." Stuart Townsend was there, speaking in the cool but confident tone of a man who expects to be called upon someday to explain the workings of the new electronic networks to congressmen and cabinet secretaries. But the hall was mainly filled with brokerages—little firms offering direct access to the market at a discount, and the opportunity to trade from either your home or one of their convenient offices. None could beat Omar's fee of $1.50 for 100 shares, but most offered competitive fees on larger trades: 1000 shares for $15 to $20.

The atmosphere was chaotic, unconvincing, and bizarrely familiar. The first Internet conferences, in 1994, were exactly like this. Everywhere you looked, there was some crackpot plan for transforming the universe. The moment you let your guard down, a publicist would begin describing a laughably lame concept that was supposed to have the executives of Fortune 500 companies alternately cowering in terror and leaping forward to offer a multimillion-dollar buy-out.

Roaming the floor and submitting to product demonstrations, I couldn't help trying to cut through the bullshit and separate the real business people, like Townsend, from the fakers, like the proprietors of the day-trading schools that offer virtual-reality market simulations designed to get neophytes accustomed to losing their shirts. But this was pointless. Perhaps better than anybody else in the building, I knew in advance what was going to happen. They were *all* going to get rich. The Internet was beaming its fortune-begetting rays down upon the retail trading industry, and the only thing these little companies had to do was stay put and suck it up. Barring full-scale economic meltdown, there was going to be plenty of payday to go around. In the middle of this frenzy, the million-dollar panel seemed almost like a distraction, a colorful side-show act that drew the rubes into the tent and made them available for slyer seductions.

All the same, the winners' secrets were what we were waiting for. When the panel was scheduled to start in the main hall, the exhibit floor emptied. There were a few minutes of mumbo jumbo and microphone-fiddling on the stage, and then, there they were: real, live million-dollar traders. The first to speak was a soft-voiced, ingenuous man about my age. He revealed that he had learned about day trading from an article in *Inc.* magazine, and he added, bravely, that he had no idea why he'd been so successful. "I've always been kind of a Renaissance man," he murmured. "Eventually you start figuring things out and, you know, make money. I really don't know exactly." This answer was shockingly honest, and I respected him for it. He bought lots of stocks, and they went higher. What more was he supposed to say?

Lawrence Black, the biggest star, faced the most pressure to embellish the truth, but he didn't flinch either. He explained that all he did was watch the market, and when stocks looked like they were rising he bought them. In one of the greatest bull markets in history, he took risks and made his fortune. Black humorously denigrated a technical approach that was too finely tuned. "Use the eyeball method on the graphs," he advised, putting his thumb in front of his face like a painter measuring a model. "Close one eye, and if it looks like it has momentum going up, then it is going up."

Later, in a quiet room off the main hall, I cornered Black and congratulated him. Taking advantage of the moment, I asked the supertrader to communicate to me personally any additional fundaments of his success. He cast a supercilious eye upon my booblike countenance. "IQ," he answered, "and experience." I am pretty sure he was being funny.

On the million-dollar panel, there were only two

traders who actually described their methods. Interestingly, neither traded Nasdaq stocks. One was a pure tape reader who traded only the same three stocks on the New York Stock Exchange. He watched his favorite indicator—the S&P 500 futures index, which gives a picture of market sentiment—and played his three stocks in short-term swings. He attempted to predict the market only two to six minutes in advance, and he made hundreds and hundreds of round-trips every day. Trading as a registered broker with a firm that is a member of the Exchange, he had extremely low costs, and since the NYSE is arranged somewhat more fairly than the Nasdaq, he didn't have to worry as much about the bad executions that plague Nasdaq traders. As far as most of the Internet fans and aspiring day traders in the audience were concerned, he might as well have been speaking Russian. "Which stocks do you trade?" somebody asked. He gave the names of three mainstream banks. Everybody agreed this was bizarre.

The second trader who was willing to go into details was even odder than the first. He was a heavyset ex-broker and ex–small businessman who was obsessed with economic realities. He described trading as "an intellectual game" and said he did homework every morning and every night. "Through becoming well-versed in many different companies," he said, "I acquired the confidence to know I can weather any trend." His obsession was identifying the best firms in various sectors, and then learning to think like the managers of the big institutional investment funds, so that he could anticipate the flow of money.

This trader's labored cadence and almost defiant realism reminded me of the some of the newspaper reporters I knew in New York who loved to beat you over the head with their encyclopedic knowledge of sports, politics, and entertainment. They could tell you the name of the last judge impeached for bribery on the municipal court, and sing you the lyrics from the finale of a Broadway stinker from the seventies, and if they put their neurotically competitive cerebrums to work picking stocks, they could probably make good money. But like his colleague Mr. Tape-Reader, Mr. Fundamentals was out of his element here at the day-trading Expo. What he was suggesting was way beyond us. It was as if he were Mark McGwire telling a room full of city-leaguers to put their weight on their back foot and keep their eyes on the ball. Well, thanks a bunch, Champ—but when do I start hitting home runs?

The trading world has been shaken by the Internet revolution. The abusive and socially exclusive system of apprenticeship at the big brokerage houses—far weaker today than decades ago for many reasons—will likely suffer a definitive collapse as low-cost executions make the markets accessible. The fundamentals guy and the fast-trading bank-stock speculator are examples of an opening in the profession for savvy players who have turned their backs on the Street. Tomorrow, when ordinary investors want to relieve themselves of some securities they've held in their retirement accounts, or stock up on a few shares for the future, they may be able to head directly to the market, where an independent operator, rather than a conventional dealer, will take the other side of their trade. The question was, where did that leave me? The market was hardly looking any easier. In fact, with so much increased competition, any faltering in the bull market seemed likely to make trading more harrowing and difficult than ever.

"It used to be like shooting fish in a barrel," admitted Oliver Velez, the cofounder of Pristine Trading. Pristine publishes a tout sheet called *The Pristine Day Trader* and is one of the leading day-trading training companies. Velez and his partner, Greg Capra, function as docents in this still-unregulated field, inaugurating the curious and warning off the unprepared. Unlike Ken Wolff, who is very direct and personal—like a psychotherapist or a flying instructor—Velez is trying to funnel new traders into the industry on a mass scale. He prides himself on his legitimacy, and tries to warn new students that, though the rewards are great, they are battling long odds. He has embarked on an ambitious program of expansion, and is branching out to Europe and Latin America.

Like most of his fellow pioneers, Velez was doing SOES trading in 1993, a year he remembers with pleasure. But he agreed with the other SOES bandits I had talked with. "This form of trading is dead," he said. In his opinion, the majority of traders today are destined to lose. His goal as a teacher is to inculcate a calm attitude about losing money, and he urged students to start with enough that they could lose plenty without going bankrupt. A starting stake of $50,000 was the bare minimum, and he was more comfortable accepting students with $100,000 or more to risk. "It's been normal for people to lose twenty-five to forty percent of their starting capital, but those losses are the rungs on the ladder of success, if handled properly," Velez told me.

At a dinner party celebrating the Expo, Velez gave a short speech to the assembled guests. "We have never been closer to the complete democratization of Wall Street," he said. "Out of the morning dew of this industry the next Goldman Sachs and the next Merrill Lynches will emerge." I knew Velez wasn't talking about me. He was talking about the companies responsible for creating the new trading infrastructure, the global electronic securities market outside the control of the Nasdaq and the NYSE.

Velez had good reason to be thrilled. The SOES traders threw themselves a party back when it was possible to buy a stock for, say, 32 and turn around and sell it for 32¾ to a slowpoke market maker whose bid was staring you right in the face. This strategy entailed almost no risk at all, and was the kind of entrepreneurial capitalism a person could really enjoy. Now that the SOES profits were gone, the race was on to build other businesses. Trading houses were attractive because the aspiring day trader will produce thousands of dollars in weekly commissions doing trades that cost brokerages a fraction of that amount. Educational enterprises were appealing because they scaled—the same materials and advice could be sold to tens or hundreds of thousands, without proportionate increases in costs. The biggest thinkers, people like Omar Amanat and Stuart Townsend, saw the entire industry's trading network up for grabs.

For the aspiring traders, Velez had a different message. Speaking in an all-American idiom that mixed business and the Bible, he recounted his own painful education in the markets. His tale encompassed bankruptcies, humiliations, multiple evictions, and periods of black despair in which he shut himself into a closet night after night. "But then," he declared, "there came a day when I knew I'd looked Satan in the eye for the last time. I didn't care if I lost my stake again. I knew I was either going to succeed in this industry or end up a bum on the street with a tin cup in one hand and a copy of *The Wall Street Journal* in the other!"

Velez's audience laughed and was inspired, for who among them really doubted their purity of heart, their strength of character, their capacity for discipline, their ability to add large numbers?

Who, that is, except for me? By the end of Velez's speech, I knew I was through. I was through because I didn't get into trading to challenge Satan. I didn't get into trading to go broke, be evicted, or lose half my savings on the ladder of success. I got into it for one reason, and for one reason alone, and I've already said what it was.

On Saturday night I sat with Harvey Houtkin for a few minutes, and he spoke with contempt about some of the reporters who had questioned him critically about

whether his customers at the All-Tech day-trading emporium were really successful. "It depends what you mean
by success," he complained. "Were they profitable? Well,
that is not the only definition of success. The guy who
trades a little bit, say an older guy, who passes the time,
finds it interesting, he might not be profitable, but he's
successful."

I liked Harvey, but this was horsepucky. I knew very
well that the guy who trades a little bit—yes, even an
older guy—wasn't in the market for a mild diversion between household chores. He wasn't trying to pass some
time on a rainy Wednesday when the triple-A game was
rained out. He was mixing it up in the pit with tens of
thousands of tough competitors for the same reason I was:
because he was hoping to take some cash out. If he *really*
wanted to make money and not lose it, he'd be focusing
his attention and redrawing his charts and keeping every
distracting person or thought away from his brain during
trading hours, and during homework hours, and during
the weekend hours when an unexpected meeting of OPEC
ministers sent energy stocks soaring in the European markets.

For some people, maybe this made sense. Phil, for instance, was a forty-year-old newspaper photographer
trapped in a dead-end job in Florida. "The paper is pinch-
ing pennies," he told me. "New technologies are taking
over. I feel like I'm working in a slide-rule factory." Phil
was too young to retire. He had been preparing for his
new trading career for a year, learning about charting and

corporate accounting and watching the market every day. He felt he would soon be ready to commit about $60,000 of savings. Phil was fascinated by the market, not for its own sake, but because it offered a chance to earn a decent income. As Phil grew older, and opportunities for break-out success in his chosen profession dwindled, day trading offered a much needed route of escape.

I wasn't nearly so desperate. While the former SOES traders were racing as fast as their legs could carry them to become Internet entrepreneurs, I was already an Internet entrepreneur. True, my Web site was small, my contributors were smart alecks, and we didn't sell many books or much pet food. But our ragged enterprise threw off enough cash to keep me in Pop Tarts, and though I tried not to let on, or get maudlin, I kind of liked it. The fact was—and it pained me to admit it—I had something to lose. I didn't want a new job, a new life, or a new religion. I just wanted my million bucks.

On the other hand, what was I willing to trade for it?

So far, I'd been lucky. I'd strolled to the edge of the market and picked up some stray thousand-dollar bills that were blowing in my direction, but when I got a good view down into the game, the action looked pretty bloody. The more honest players, if you caught them at one of their more honest moments, would warn you that apprentices must be prepared to relinquish a lot of cash—even all of it—in learning. And there was something more. You had to humbly devote yourself to the market—like a pilgrim, like a saint; or worse, like a really hard worker.

I scratched my head, amazed at what I was thinking. I was thinking: *What do I get in return for all this devotion?* And the answer I kept coming up with was: *Only money.* And not an infinite amount of money, either; not magical strings of zeros angling away toward the vanishing point like the undying moan of a cartoon drunk. The market—maybe, if I behaved myself—would give me something to work with, but hardly enough to dream with.

All the same, I should admit that I haven't taken CNBC off the favorites list of my universal remote. I can still whistle the theme songs. And sometimes, even today, in the predawn hours, I give a start and sit straight up in my bed and ask myself, honestly wondering: *Am I a millionaire yet?*

GLOSSARY

ask: The amount of money a seller demands for a share of stock. An ask is sometimes called an offer. (See SPREAD.)

bid: The amount of money a buyer will pay for a share of stock. (See SPREAD.)

ECN: An ECN is an electronic communications network used to trade stocks. The term encompasses SelectNet, the official Nasdaq ECN, which is owned by the National Association of Securities Dealers; an important private ECN called Instinet, which is used by large institutional investors; and a handful of private ECNs, such as Island and Archipelago, which are used by day traders. The owners of the new ECNs hope and believe that ordinary retail investors will soon be buying and selling stocks directly on the ECNs, without going through a dealer. Major brokerage firms have responded to this threat by making heavy investments in several new ECNs, which they now partially own.

execution: Trades are complicated rituals that involve signaling prices, accepting offers, confirming purchases, and accounting for money transferred. Taken as a whole, this process is called the execution.

float: The float is the number of shares in a company that are available for trading by the public. In many firms, a relatively small number of investors, executives, and employees own much of the stock, leaving only a small percentage free for outsiders to trade. Limited supply means that low-float stocks can be very volatile.

gap: A gap occurs when a stock opens at a price significantly higher or lower than the closing price the previous day. A gap up means that buying pressure has been building overnight. A gap down means that owners have become discouraged and are eager to escape.

Greater Fool Theory: The Greater Fool Theory is a longstanding hypothesis about the value of corporate securities. An essay for Suck rehearsing some of the stories we have told here attracted a letter that clearly outlined this theory. The letter's writer, Walter Frederick Bauer, has given us permission to print it:

> If you get an MBA in finance, you will be exposed to many theories of stock valuation. The easiest one to understand is called the Gordon model. It states that a

stock is worth the present value of the future income derived from its dividend stream. You can throw in the present value of the stock when you sell it, too, if you like. The models get more and more arcane, with such baroque variants as the Efficient Frontier portfolio theory discounting stock value for risk and so forth. But if your professors aren't totally afflicted with academic cephalo-anal impaction, towards the end of the course they will tell you, as mine did, what the real stock valuation model is, and the name says it all.

It's called The Greater Fool Theory.

First the premises: (1) Anybody who buys a stock that has defaulted on a dividend is a fool. (2) Anybody who buys a stock that has never paid a dividend is a greater fool. (3) Anybody who buys a stock that has never paid a dividend and has a price/earnings ratio indicating that its return on investment is inferior to putting the money in an essentially risk-free Treasury bill is an even greater fool (note that stock in a company that has never made any money at all has an infinite P/E ratio, indicating the infinite suckerdom of those who buy it). (4) Fools who buy stocks like that are counting on a still even greater fool to buy it from them at a higher price some time in the future (nobody, not even a fool, buys a stock because they think its price will decline). (5) Fools like that are all over the place and far outnumber rational investors. (6) Fools are motivated only by fear and greed. (7) Fools drive the stock market.

Now, just by sheer random chance, some fools will walk away with huge piles of other fools' money. And still other fools will conclude that the fools with that money are geniuses, buy their books and lectures, subscribe to their Web sites, and try to emulate them. The Greater Fool Theory implies that as long as there are fifth-, fourth-, third- and second-order fools to buy dotcom stocks at higher prices from the first-order fools who bought them in some fool's paradise of an IPO frenzy, then Mark O. Barton will remain an aberration. He will be nothing more than a weak, pathetic person with a sick mind and decayed character—a moral degenerate who could not accept or cope with the risk of total, bankrupt failure, a risk that every fool in the stock market should be prepared to accept and cope with.

Now for the catch: there can be no shortage of supply when the valued objects in question are stocks in companies that have never made a dime. Therefore, the shortage, sooner or later, always turns out to be in the supply of fools.

This is essentially what happened in 1929. Back then, some fool confronting the consequences of his folly would do the gentlemanly thing and jump out a window. Today, in gun-queer, everybody's-a-victim, the-world-owes-me-big-time, post-modern America, they aren't gentlemen and they won't be jumping. They'll be locking, loading and spraying hot lead.

Because it wasn't supposed to be like this—they were supposed to get filthy rich, quick and easy, and be surrounded by shiny toys and pricey real estate and envious admirers, and if it isn't happening, then somebody must be to blame. The damn fool they bought that nose-diving, toilet-tanking Internet stock from, for instance. And what about the rest of them—(that's you, me and the woman with the kid who just walked in to ask for directions)—they're in on it too, aren't they? Take it from an MBA in finance: learn how to duck and be in shape to run like hell.

IPO: When a company is "taken public" with an initial public offering (IPO), few or no shares are sold directly to retail customers. Rather, the banking firm responsible for managing the IPO sells large blocks of shares to big investors. The bank takes a chunk, too. These initial investors get the shares at the "offering price," which conventionally ranges from $10 to $25. A stock that goes public at an offering price of $15 may begin trading on the first day at a much higher price. In the heyday of Internet mania, it has been common to see a stock begin trading at many times its offering price, and then immediately start falling as the big investors and the investment bank take wonderful profits.

limit offer: For ordinary retail investors, a limit order is an order to a broker to buy or sell stock at a specified price. There often seem to be lots of trades when a stock hits a whole number. Day traders assume—perhaps correctly— that this is caused by brokers executing limit orders for their customers.

long: Long is the opposite of short. It is a noun and an adjective, but never a verb. Longs are buyers of stocks. They are hoping that the price will go up. The public is generally unaware of the possibility of selling stocks you do not own (shorting); therefore they make money in bull runs and lose them in corrections. This has given rise to the speculator's commonplace, "The sucker is always long." Speculators, of course, will also try to get long during a bull run.

margin: Margin is money for buying stocks made available as a loan from your broker. Interest is charged on the loan. The securities you buy serve as collateral. If share prices fall, the collateral loses value, and your broker will demand cash to make up the difference; this is known as a margin call. Government regulations limit the amount of money brokers can lend customers. In the pre-crash era, customers could buy stocks from their brokers with only 10 percent of their own money. This means that if the price of their shares fell by more than 10 percent, their broker would issue a margin call, demanding more cash. Bankruptcy could arrive in an instant.

market maker: A market maker in the Nasdaq market is a dealer who pledges to provide liquidity by taking the other side of your trades. Traditionally, when you want to buy or sell a Nasdaq stock, you buy or sell it from a market maker. Often there is an additional intermediary known as an order-entry firm who will take your order and provide customer service while passing the trade itself to the market maker. Web brokers, such as E*Trade, are order-entry firms. Market makers, which include big brokerage firms, attracted enormous criticism in the mid-nineties for fixing prices. Though they adamantly denied the charges at first, they eventually paid a settlement of about a billion dollars.

momentum: When a stock rises, it often attracts interest and rises more. Or the opposite happens: the increase in price makes share owners want to realize their profits, so they sell. Then the selling makes the price fall back again, which frightens people, and the price falls more. The gyrations and undulations and spasms of a stock over the course of an hour or a day are not easily predictable, but many traders try. Technical analysis of short-term stock movement is sometimes known as momentum analysis. Perhaps this is because stocks seem to have a quality very loosely analogous to physical inertia: when they are moving, they often stay moving. Short-term stock prices display a weird behavior unknown to physical objects, however. While a rapidly moving stock is more likely than a slowly moving stock to continue to move rapidly, the *direction* of this movement appears to be arbitrary.

penny stock: A penny stock is a low-priced stock that is not listed on a major exchange such as the New York Stock Exchange or Nasdaq. High in both risk and volatility, penny stocks are popular among speculators who enjoy owning tens of thousands of shares, and who have great faith. A penny stock seldom sells for a penny. Sometimes it sells for many pennies. There are even penny stocks that sell for several dollars.

position: A position is a commitment of money in a market speculation. When you take a long position, you buy shares. When you take a short position, you sell shares that you will later have to buy back. When you have sold all your stocks and covered all your shorts, you have no positions.

price-to-earnings ratio: The price-to-earnings ratio is a common method of tracking the value of stocks. The price is the price of shares. The earnings are the company's profits. Since many Internet companies have no profits, the price-to-earnings ratio is of little use in establishing their worth.

print: This old-fashioned term refers to the public acknowledgment of a trade. When you see bids or asks flashing by on your screen but no prints, it means that the bids or asks are being canceled before they are executed.

pump-and-dump: This is a classic technique of money-making that involves promoting the prospects of a company whose shares you own, then secretly selling your shares into the buying interest you created. It is very difficult to do this with a well-known, widely traded company; there are too many shares outstanding and too much information flowing for any individual to have an effect. But a smaller company with only a few hundred thousand shares available can be easily moved by an experienced and savvy manipulator, particularly if that person is an executive of the company, in control of press releases and other eagerly watched omens of fortune. Speculators outside the company often try to get a stock to run by hyping it to a circle of devotees who then spread out through the online discussion boards and create ripples, and even waves. TokyoJoe was once asked about whether he made money this way and he answered, with impressive cynicism: "Pump-and-dump? Who *isn't* a pump-and-dump?"

short: Short can be a verb, noun, or adjective. As a verb, it means to sell stocks you have borrowed, in the hope that you will be able to buy them back later ("cover your short") at a better price. As a noun, it refers to a speculator with one or more short positions or with a regular strategy of short-selling. Shorts bet on a downturn in prices, and since shorting a stock means selling it, the act of shorting can, at sufficient volume, cause a drop in price. This makes shorts unpopular among people who hope the price will rise. As an adjective, it simply refers to the state of being short, as in the sentence: "Don't listen to anything he says—he's short."

SOES: The Small Order Execution System (SOES) was created in 1984 to automatically execute small trades. Most trades in Nasdaq stocks were executed only when accepted by a dealer; SOES automatically made the trade at the dealer's posted price. When the market was moving, a dealer who did not update a price could "get SOESed." In other words, a SOES order would automatically buy or sell shares from the dealer at the (now) inferior price. This created new opportunities for "SOES bandits" like Harvey Houtkin. SOES still exists, and is used by day traders, but the opportunities to take money from dealers have diminished. The game has become crowded, and dealers are better about updating their prices. There is a long and complicated history of changing SOES rules that is of little interest now that day traders have multiple other channels for interacting directly with the market.

split: A stock split is an accounting maneuver that doubles the number of shares and cuts the price in half. (There are also three-for-one splits that triple the supply and cut the price by two thirds.) In following the flight path of a booming stock, you have to adjust for splits to experience proper amazement. Here's how you do it: First, pick a starting date; note the stock price; pick the ending date; then cut the price in half for every two-for-one split between the starting date and the ending date. If you purchased an Internet stock for 20 and the stock split six times since you bought it (you didn't, we know, but *if* you did), it is as if the price you paid was a little more than 31 cents per share. This is known as the split-adjusted price. If you sold at 10 (you didn't, we know, but *if* you did) your profit was more than 9 per share.

spread: The spread is the difference between the amount a seller is asking for a share of stock and the amount a buyer is bidding for it. The spread provides a rich vein of profit for professional dealers in stocks. The Nasdaq market, for many years, was structured to ensure that there would always be a dealer on either side of a retail trade. When you bought a stock, you bought it at the *dealer's* ask. When you sold it, you sold it at the *dealer's* bid. Only with the advent of electronic communications networks (ECNs) have some retail customers (day traders, mainly) begun to trade with each other directly.

stop: A stop is usually a limit order that will get you out of a position at a prearranged price. If you are long, a stop will sell your shares if they fall to a certain price. If you are short, a stop will "buy to cover" if shares rise to a certain price. For day traders, stops are usually just promises to themselves to get out of a position if it goes against them. Since a day trader's stop is merely a self-promise, it is frequently broken.

volatility: Volatility is a measure of how much and how quickly a stock changes price. To day traders, volatility is a good thing, because a stock that runs up and down quickly provides frequent opportunities for profit.

INDEX

ABOUT THE AUTHORS

JOEY ANUFF (joey@suck.com) is cofounder and editor-in-chief of Suck.com, the Web's pioneering daily humor Web site. He lives in San Francisco.

GARY WOLF (gw@aether.com) is a regular contributor to *Wired* and other magazines and the author of the forthcoming book *Bengali Typhoon: The Rise and Fall of Wired Ventures.* He lives in San Francisco.

ABOUT THE TYPE

This book was set in Melior, a typeface designed by Hermann Zapf and released by the Stempel foundry in 1952. With square serifs and condensed proportions, it has a highly legible and elegant design.